T0064586

LOVE LETTERS TO
AMERICA

LESA K. SMITH

authorHOUSE®

AuthorHouse™ LLC
1663 Liberty Drive
Bloomington, IN 47403
www.authorhouse.com
Phone: 1-800-839-8640

Published by AuthorHouse   03/28/2014

ISBN: 978-1-4918-6906-2 (sc)
ISBN: 978-1-4918-6904-8 (hc)
ISBN: 978-1-4918-6907-9 (e)

New King James Version Copyright @1979, 1980, 1982 by Thomas Nelson Inc.

English Standard Version (EVS) Copyright 2001by Crossway

In dedication to my Mom and Dad who took, raised and loved me enough to teach me about Jesus and His love. To my brothers Bill and Scott, who loved me and made my life wonderful growing up. The times we had were some of the greatest times in my life! To my husband and children, you are the fun and joy of my life. I thank My God for such earthly treasures that have sweetened and added brightness to my life.

CONTENTS

INTRODUCTION

Please allow me to introduce myself to you. I am Lesa Smith and I am a baby boomer in the prime of life. Before I was aware of my own existence, I had real needs. First of all, I was born without a real home. My God cared for me, when I could not care for myself. Quite simply, I am one who owes Him everything! I was born to parents who could not care for me. By the time I was three, my birth mother had died. However, God's plan for my life was already in full swing. I was situated in a family that God made especially for me. I had a hard working Dad and a Mom who stayed at home with us. That's right I was also given a brother too! I had been given a home and my parents had their God given family. You can imagine, I am very much Pro Life and Pro Adoption too. I see it as God's perfect answer to one of life's toughest situations. As I share my heart, I will also share some of my life with you. God has had His hand on me! It is a clear picture to see and a story that needs to be told. May reading my story inspire you towards your own walk, in the Truth. Remember God's Truth in your life, will set you free. God is ALIVE AND WELL! I want to share with you, His involvement in my life . . .

It is with a heart of great concern and love that I share in strong language, the written pages of this book. In many ways some of what I am saying, is on the hearts of most Americans. I am taking the time to say it, for all of us. My intent is not to pass judgment in any way that is only for God. I am in hopes of making a connection with you and challenging each of you, to positive action. If this book provokes you to growing, introspection and action, it has served it purpose. As you read, please check out the wonderful Scriptures from God's Word all along the way. It will help you to grow in your love for God. Then, as you are blessed, please share this work with another that is in need. I believe that God will minister and move through the Bible Scriptures to help those who need a positive Word from Him. In the busy world that we live in, it is the best that I can do, to try and get your attention. You can love me, disagree with me or this is America, even debate me. I welcome your interaction, as you read this book. I am hoping that you will find my Eternal God and His plan to rescue you. His door is always open! His heart is always turned toward you! There is nothing that He desires more than for you to walk through His open door to Him. The closer that you are to Him, the happier you both will be!

THE PERIL OF AMERICA'S KIDS

It was May 15, 1958, beautiful spring day in Tennessee. It was Mother's day and Mom could not have been more excited! The day had finally come, for her family to be completed. This was the day that the Lord added me, the long awaited daughter, to the family. In many ways, I had the classic American up-bringing. My life consisted of church, school and neighborhood friends. It was a time when walking neighborhood streets was safe. My friends and I walked everywhere. We walked several miles to Kay's Ice Cream, for a hamburger and shake. It was a favorite Saturday walk for me. In my free time, when I got out of the house, there were many adventures for me. One family in particular stands out. It was my best friend Cindy and her sister's, Sandy and Debbie. They were like sisters to me. They were my dance and swimming partners. They taught me about dating, hair and make up. Other fun memories were that of climbing trees, eating green apples and hide and seek. There were times when I got stuck in the tree tops. Other times, we would launch balloon and apple fights from there. I loved to skate and had a board. I did my fair share of bicycling too. My brother was better at alot of things, than I was. I can remember rainy days, the radio and playing cards. He still tries to teach me to this day. Close to home was a playground at a Catholic school. We spent our fair share of time over there, playing and talking.

My Dad was a carpenter. He could build anything! He took our four room house and made it into a split level. I can still remember going through the plastic, to see the studs of my bedroom walls. Dad was strict on me and Mom was the lenient one. One of Dad's rules was that I had to be home before the street lights came on. That was one rule I don't recall breaking at all! Dad worked out of town a lot. In the summers when he was gone, things were really laid back in ease.

My Mom was always at home with us. She cooked everything under the sun. I grew up with a true appreciation for home cooked meals. I still follow her example, as I cook for my family today. Rin Tin Tin and family hobo dinners, were favorite evenings. Captain Kangaroo greeted us in the morning, as we downed our cereal or pop tarts. Lassie and Andy Griffith were some of my favorite shows. My Mom always made sure, my brother and I were in church. God encountered me there. That encounter would forever change my life. Growing up was wholesome and good. In many ways, it was some of the happiest times of my life. I would think that many baby boomers can relate to this kind of childhood memories. However, it is with a heart of concern that I compare this picture, with the typical home life of some children today. Many children today are experiencing radically different, home life realities. There are the latch key kids, in the broken homes that have little to no supervision, after school. Or, the single parents, the mother or dad, who is trying to play both roles, in another stress filled reality. What about the kids born addicted to drugs, because of their parents own addictions? What quality of life, do they really have? Who will care enough to rescue them? What about the kids in foster homes, that are being constantly shifted around. For some of these kids their only value, is for the chores and income, that they bring to the family. Who will show love to them? We all know about the kids in the hood that have witnessed crimes and death. Violence and death is a past time of the drug dealers and the gangs that walk their streets. Who cares enough to go to them and show God's love?

Today, America recognizes fulfilling the role of Super Mom, can come with over-whelming demands. Many are still trying to burn candles at both ends. They have yet to realize that their wick is about all used up, as it flickers dimly with fatigue. The stress of doing it all, comes with a price. Stress, fatigue, short tempers and illness could be showing signs, of the faltering. I know that there are many moms that are super and successful, in homes today. Ignoring the reality of others who struggle denies that there are needs all around us. There are so many homes in America that would benefit from an act of kindness. The worth of a positive role model has a priceless impact, on a child who struggles. Think for a moment about the child you know, who sits and thinks no one loves them. Could it be that the business of your life, never gives you time, to even consider such realities? Pre-occupation with our own lives, can be blinding to us. When we can not see, we will certainly miss out on acts of service and love to others, who need us. Just for a moment, consider all of the children in the world who have waited in silence and suffering, for someone to come and show that they care. Is it possible that no one ever came, because it was YOU that God had to impact their lives? That is the very meaning of the word tragedy. James 1:27 says this, "Religion that God our Father accepts as pure and faultless is this, to look after orphans and widows in their distress and to keep oneself from being polluted by the world." How can we really say that we love God, if the busy in our lives is never ending. And when we look, we have lived our lives in ignorance of our fellow man and his needs.

THE ADOPTION OPTION

I was adopted by parents, who wanted their "little girl" as much as their son. I have been given, a special outlook on the adoption process and unwed mothers. My Mom wanted a little girl so much, that she made continual calls to our case worker, to see how much longer it would be. I found out that I was a special case, as I was almost a year old when my parents got me. In the 50's, you could still get babies very easily. Mom had so much enthusiasm, that when the time came for me to join them, God had a special treat in store for her! I joined my new family on my Mom's birthday, as well as Mother's day. I guess you could say, I was probably the best birthday present, she was ever given!

There are millions of families trying to adopt today. A great deal of the children, are now coming from outside the United States. The wait for a child can be years in the making. Only God knows how many children have died to abortion. The whole question is one that I will always struggle with, as an adoptee. You see, I believe that one family's heartbreak is another families, answer from God. The Bible plainly tells us, that God is in the process of creation of life, in the mother's womb. Psalm 139:13 "You formed my inward parts; you covered me in my mother's womb." God is totally aware of the conception of every life, in the mother's womb and He has a plan for that life! Even conception in the secret places, does not miss the eye of God. God, the Creator of Life holds all life as precious to Him! What we don't find, is the unacceptable conditions deemed by man, for birth. My heart can't help but wonder, if as a society, we have thrown away some of our greatest people. Have we just simply tossed away, some of the greatest blessings that God had in store for our nation? There is no higher concept for our purpose, than God's hand on our life, even before we were born! The Bible plainly says that man is made in the image of God. Therefore, we must not accept any belief that damages our self-esteem and calls us, useless or unlovable. There is One Who's eye, has always been on us and calls our life precious in His sight!

As I have wrestled with the abortion clinics and the American home, one recurrent theme comes to mind; the circle of condemnation, pride and embarrassment. Christians and non-Christians alike can get caught up in the destructive cycle that leads to the death of a child. I recognize the tactic of the, Garden of Eden . . . "Let's cover it up." It still plays today. The theory about our children of . . . "I did it right" . . . crashes and burns right before parent's eyes. The hopes and dreams for their child, is in jeopardy. Many times the child is too young or immature, to take on the responsibilities of a baby. Or, what about the child that is an achiever? He or she has everything going for them. It would be a shame, to alter the progress of their life. Both of these examples are excellent reasons to consider the adoption option. Young mothers that are living in struggling broken homes and poverty, should consider the best way for the child. I have heard it said, that it is "not cool" to put your child up for adoption. To that I would say, "Their are millions of grown children, who praise God for the sacrifice, their mothers made for them." That self sacrificing act of love, gave them the most wonderful opportunity of a life time. To have two loving parents to nurture and provide for a stable home. Giving up a child is one of the hardest decisions to make. But keeping a child when you are not prepared is by far the hardest road to take. When you release your child to the loving arms of the adoptive parents, you can be sure that your child is loved and wanted. The perspective parents have been interviewed and investigated. They have completed the home study by an adoption official. As I think about this process, it takes me back to the story of a couple from church. They are one of the most humble and loving couples, I have ever known. He is an engineer and she is a nurse. They had one child together and she had miscarried, another five. Because of certain health circumstances, their chance of having other children was over. But, her heart kept echoing that there was to be other children. After seeking God's guidance, they turned to the adoption option. The wait had started for the next little family member. They were a praying couple and the church also prayed for them. Finally, the day came and God gave them a little brother for Paul. Everyone rejoiced over the special little life that God had given them. In a way, he was given to all of us!

Here in Knoxville, a woman who wishes to place her child for adoption can have a hand in selecting their child's future family. She is given all the important information about the family and has pictures to see as well. A young woman is given several portfolios and is allowed to select the future parents. I can remember when my friends got the call, that they had been selected. Excitement and elation filled the air for all of us.

An adopted child is welcome by a host of other family members, when they are placed in a Christian home. They are anticipated by the whole church. It is a time of celebration in the hearts of the proud parents and their extended family. We all marveled at the special gift of love that God sent to our special friends. We know that God has a very special plan for everyone, when He does this. A plan that includes many loving friends, in the church family.

I like the approach of the portfolios, where a young women is given the opportunity to review important information, such as career and religious preference. And, is able to see pictures of physical characteristics. I want to challenge all states to think about this alternative idea. This way is somewhat creative and would be comforting to the natural mother. She could have a sense of peace, knowing that she was able to pick the life that she wanted for her child. She would carry with her the comfort of knowing the arrangements, she had been able to make. She has been given a springboard of promise and hope, for her child. She can imagine in a positive way, the life of her child, as she finds the strength to let go in love. I believe this would assist her to being able to find comfort and peace, in her situation.

With the abortion rate so high in America, the issue is not that a young girl is pregnant or has made a mistake; simply because we all have make mistakes. We must not speak condemnation on her head, lest we find that what we speak, we too are deserving of such a judgment. The Bible says, we fulfill God's Laws, as we practice love. If we are called to love our enemies, how much more should we practice love towards the young girl in trouble. We must stop the condemnation of her. We must practice guidance and love that can only be found with God's help. Deut. 30:19 says it this way, "I have set before you life and death, blessing and cursing; therefore choose life, that both you and your descendants may live!"

To all loving Moms and Dads, I would tell you when you lead your child down the road to abortion you sentence them to a life long process, of mourning and regret. A process that they will be working on, far after the things of yesterday, have been put to bed. It is a piece of the puzzle of their lives that they can never reclaim. An act to which they surely must wonder, if they will have to face, as they stand before God. One thing that may never die is the conscious awareness of a death that has occurred, at their hands. In the hard time of unplanned pregnancy, I challenge you to find in the Word of God, that the death of a child is the right way. Instead, be people of good conscience and love. Do the right thing by an unborn child, who would very much like to live and find God. Walk through the process with your child, holding the hand of God. In faith and trust surrender your helpless little one. Then know, that you and your child can have peace, because your little one, found life on earth. Instead of regret, you can spend the rest of your life praying for the little one, that you lovingly released. You can know that we have a loving Heavenly Father, who hears us and will engage the child that you pray for! Why? Simply because you were obedient and chose life and He is a God Who loves us all! Oh, that you may know, that God would have us to walk in obedience to Him, so that we may have peace of heart and mind. God tells us that we will reap that which we sow. For a harvest of peace to rest on your family, we must make the only choice that honors God, the Authority Of All Life and choose life!

GOD'S PROMISE TO ALL
UNBORN CHILDREN

From the times of ancient mankind until today, we see in individuals, the replaying of the same old mistakes. Father Abraham and Sarah made the mistake of trying to rush God's promise of having a child, by taking Hagar the maid servant. We know the story well. Instead of waiting on God to fulfill the promise of a child, they took matters into their own hands. The results were disastrous. Sarah began to hate Hagar, jealousy and strife arose. Things came to a boiling point and Sarah sent her away. Hagar was run out of the camp. As Hagar ran, she no doubt was afraid, confused and angry. She was fleeing the hostility of her situation. We find her crying in Gen. 21:16. This scene is of primary importance and we all should take note of it. In Gen. 16:9 God sends an angel to personally encounter Hagar. His message to her is to return in submission to Sarah, to her place in the camp. He proceeds to tell her, that God has a plan for the life of her unborn child. His name was to be called Ishmael, which means, "God hears." He was to be the father of the Arab people. God is never defeated by our sin, nor is He caught off guard. He knows of all things, before they are in existence. As I look at Hagar, I see the plight of all unwed mothers. The fear, running away and hopelessness, that can try to peer in the window of her heart. I believe this is an eternal spiritual picture of the young unwed mother running away. We see the Faithful and True God, supernaturally intervening bringing a message of calm reassurance and purpose, to an otherwise tragic ending. Maybe you are an unwed teen, who finds yourself under the condemnation of your family and friends. If you will open your heart today to the Word of God, you can have with certainty the same promise of hope, for the future of your child. Our God is a God of hope, who promises to meet us where ever we find ourselves, with reassurance and a plan. Our God is the Author and Creator of all life. He is for life. Young women you can rest assured that our God wants to comfort and bless you and your children. Take heed, God still loves you and has a plan and purpose, for you both!

As Godly parents and friends, it is our job to receive the story of Hagar too. We must mirror God, by encouraging life. As parents, you can in love acknowledge the wrong doing and disappointment you feel, without running your child out of the camp. You can have peace knowing that God always has a plan. You can honor God by choosing life and letting your light shine, by having faith in this difficult time. As a Christian nation our decision must be to let our children live. Our choice must not be to kill and destroy our innocent young!

THE QUESTION OF TO TELL
OR NOT TO TELL?

Out of the special circumstances of adoption arises the age old question for the adoptive parents, "Do we tell him or her?" Although, I know that adoptive parents love their children with all of their hearts, my vote sides with having a time of truth with your special child. It can be a time of wrangling about all of the details of what to tell and when, what to say and not say. I am sure in the hearts of these special parents, there comes a time of temptation of, "not to tell!" The bonding and history of love makes them want to shield their child, from any possible hurt. The love that is between them is just like that of a natural born child. Although, this temptation is understandable, I whole-heartedly believe it is not the wise path for the family. To withhold information from a child about their identity may result in a dangerous game of trust and betrayal. Children being innocent, have complete trust in you, as their parents. Absolute honesty will help to ensure that the trust of your love will remain. I want to share with you the details of how my parents handled this delicate matter. My reason for sharing is to assist you to find your way thru, what may be a hard process that is lacking for words. I believe that my parents are to be commended. They did it right! I know that you can too!

I don't even remember a time, when I didn't know that I was adopted. I grew up with the idea. I don't remember how old I was, when Mom told me that I was adopted. My Mom made sure, I knew that I was special and chosen by them for their family. My parents did address the fact, that I did have another family. They did not hide that from me. When they talked about my parents, they always spoke of them, in a positive light. They reassured me that, "I came from good people!" Then, Mom explained that, "They just could not keep me." "They could not take care of me." I was the kind of child that would ask intermittent questions of my Mom, about them. I always remember having a good feeling about myself, because I knew that I came from good people! See how important the truth is! My parents were wise. They knew that deep inside of me, I would some how in time, identify myself with my roots. So, they were careful to plant, good roots inside of me. I think it is so tragic when parents plant negative and harmful ideas about each other. You must remember, you are planting in a child at the emotional level and some day harmful results may root in the hearts and minds, of your beloved child.

One day when I was a little older, Mom sat me down and informed me about my biological family. She told me that I had brothers and sisters. I will never forget this experience. It was like Mom had taken a magic wand and hit me with fairy dust! That night when I went to bed, I can remember being especially mindful of them. I wondered where they were? Which state it might be? Did they ever look for me? Or, did they even remember me? I was familiar with the family concept. "I loved my brother Bill with all of my heart!"

You must tell a child the truth about their roots. Deception about something so important as their identity, can be a very costly mistake. The worst thing that can happen to a child is for everyone to know, except them. Never allow a child to get so old, that school mates could be the one to tell them something so personal. Your life with them has cocooned into a warm and safe place. Never gamble with outsiders having the rights to crush the reality of that safe and loving place. Children have the amazing talent to understand. Especially, when love supreme has the rule of their life with you and positive affirmation is involved, all along the way. I grew up being able to say that my Mom and Dad wanted me, as much as my biological family! I was a part of two good families! I was a treasure indeed!

Many years later, my Mom would say to me, "When you find your brothers and sisters, I want to meet them." It was a commissioning for me. Several years later I would find my biological family. You can imagine my surprise, when I was told about the family problems that existed, in my birth family. Things such as alcoholism, possible bank robbery and prison time for my Dad. The only good picture I have of him, is where he was arrested! But, my roots went deep with positive affirmations and I was unscathed by all of it. It was almost unbelievable for me and I found myself laughing it off. My whole experience with adoption was a very positive one. Being told the facts of the matter, simply had no consequence to me. I had been loved, sheltered and protected by Mom and Dad. I was raised to love my "birth family" and myself. "We were good." As it turned out, no one could change that for me!

Parents, I challenge you to encourage adoption for your unwed children. It is the best available opportunity, for an unplanned child. The giving away of a child is a loving self-sacrificing gesture. It is not so unlike, what Christ did for us. In love, He gave Himself sacrificially, so that we might have a more abundant life. Palms 139 says that He is at the center of all created life. We are assured that He is ready with a plan for each day of a little one's life. Will you entrust that child to Him? Give a child life. Let them be the fulfillment of a higher plan, than even you can begin to comprehend. In doing so, you will be a blest partner in the fulfillment of another's "dreams of the heart." This is in short, the very meaning of the word adoption!

THE CALL OF CRISIS

The question remains, what do you do when the dreaded call comes? "Mom and Dad Jackie is pregnant." It is quite normal to feel every emotion known to man. But, this is one time that emotion cannot lead the process. It is certainly a time to remember, that our God knows every detail of your life. God is never caught off guard by the circumstances, in our lives. He will certainly guide you, especially when life takes unexpected turns! With the abortion rate so high, it is a noble act to allow the innocent, unborn child to live. Although the way may not be easy, God will provide for everyone involved. At this critical time, choose to surround yourself with family who loves you and those who are your true friends. You will quickly learn who really loves you and will be there for you. Let life go on. Stay on call and watch for opportunities, to help those in need. Remember God is pleased, when we help others. It is a service that is as rendered unto Him, when you choose to love those who are in pain or need. Loving acts must rule in difficult times; especially if you are a child of God. If you think that you are not obligated, you would do well to take a fresh look at the Cross. The Cross reminds us, that our obligation is to love others at all times.

Where you find yourself, is no surprise to God. He, being all knowing, already has a plan in store for your family. The key is to come to Him in honesty. Allow Him, to work on your pain and even your temptations, at such a serious time. If you will make choices that honor God, even if it means standing alone, there will come a time, when you will be glad that you did. Peace always is the by product of living our lives in harmony, with the will of God. Where you find yourself, God will meet you and make provisions for all of you! The real questions is, will you allow God to? In trying times like this, your carnal nature will try to take over. You may find yourself battling with pride or a feeling of failure. These emotions are normal. However, listening to these voices, can lead you down the wrong path. Remember, you have the rest of your life to live out, the choices that you will make here. I believe with all of my heart, that it takes integrity, trust and the love of God, to allow yourself to walk in the will of God, at such a time. You can be an example, of Christ's love, when you choose life and to walk it out by faith. A clear example, for other families who will certainly follow. Life so sweet and pure is a gift from our Almighty Father. He trusts you to love Him enough, to do the right thing. In who's eyes, are you trying to find favor? I am in hopes that it will be Our Heavenly Father's . . . the One who entrusted you with a such a precious gift from above. May you walk your days out and mirror His love!

CHOOSE TO WALK IN
LORDSHIP AND HIS LOVE

In today's world people are asking, "What is my purpose here?" I believe with all of my heart, we are here to love, help, encourage and lift up others. We are to show them the love of God and to love God, with all of our hearts and minds. In doing so, we will mirror to the world that our God lives and help lead them to Him. Our time on earth may very well be a training field to prepare us to live in eternity with our God. Yes, our trials tests us; but they also build into our core character Godly attributes that could otherwise be absent. They are the chaffing salts that groom us to Christ Likeness in this world. Only God knows the exact prescription that will result in yielding His transformation, in our being.

One of the most important decisions that we can make for Christ is Lordship. Showing Christ's love means our yielding to His Will and control over our lives. As Christians we must realize that we are carrying Jesus in our bodies. Therefore, we must conduct ourselves in ways that will not grieve His Presence within us. (Eph. 4:30) God's Word tells us in the book of Ephesians to put off our old man of sin and shame and put on the new man which was created according to God, in true righteousness and holiness. (Eph. 4: 22-24) How do we do this, you might wonder? I know that I certainly have asked the same of God. His reply was this, "How did you accept My Son?" My answer was, "by faith!" Bingo! As partakers of the Word, we take a hold of the Promises of God by the accepting of Truth in the Word by faith/believing it, in our hearts. When we accept His Words of Truth in our hearts by faith, God can then spring it to life in our being! The book of Ephesians is a great place to start discovering the contrast of the old life with the new life that Christ died to give to us. You will discover much about what pleases God and how we are to walk on earth with Him. The book of Romans, Chapters 5-8 echo more of the same instructions; to help us walk in holiness and have a life pleasing unto Him. If you want a better understanding and a changed life, I challenge you to read these passages. These passages in Romans have certainly changed my life. Another Verse that puts us right on the target of blessing is Matthew 6: 33. "But seek first the Kingdom of God and His righteousness, and all these things shall be added to you." What a power group of Words! We need to be sure that we are in a relationship with our Beloved Christ and we have put Him and His Kingdom in first place over our lives. I really wonder, if practicing the exact opposite is why we are not experiencing His Presence, Power and Blessing. Our commitment to Him must be more than just a Sunday morning affair. It should show up in the way we live our lives out daily to the watching world. It should show in our words, attitude and actions. We should be reflecting His Love, His Concerns and His Agenda in this lost and dying world around us. Our hearts and minds should be set on bringing Him clearly into focus, to those who need Him, by modeling His Love. He should be showing, as we bring Him Glory by the way we live, love and help others.

The tongue is mentioned as a powerful instrument in the Bible. It is one that can be used to build others up or bring dishonor to the Name of God, by the way we use it. The Scriptures says it this way, "Out of the same mouth proceeds blessing and curses. My brethren, these things ought not to be so." "Does a spring send forth fresh water and bitter from the same opening? Can a fig tree my brethren, bear olives, or a grapevine bear figs? Thus no spring yields both salt water and fresh." (James 3: 10-12) Our call is to honor God with all of our members. This should show by what we say, how we live, what we do and monitoring our attitudes in our hearts. We can not walk in discord with others and please God. God is a God of Peace. We can not live our lives any way we choose and please God. That is not Lordship. John 15:9 says, "As the Father Loved Me, I also have Loved you, abide in My Love. If you keep my Commandments you will abide in my Love, just as I have kept My Father's Commandments and abide in His Love."

Of all the most important things in life, Love is the most important goal to achieve. Hebrews 6:10, "God is not unjust; He will not forget your work and the love that you have shown Him, as you have helped His people and continue to help them." When we show love to others, we demonstrate that we have a heart of love for God. I also know that the opposite is true. Our lack of love and the mistreatment of others, reflects our lack of true love for God. God's Word makes it clear, that God is watching us. God promises to reward His children, who walk in love. We may not see such rewards here, but they await us, in our heavenly home. Love is the most powerful ingredient, in all of life! The Love of Christ is transforming, when it is felt by others who need it. If we really want to please God with our lives, we must be filled and over flowing with His love. A life that is lived in love fulfills the Word of God. The walking out of love, in our lives demonstrates that Our GOD IS . . . . to the watching world, searching for answers. Will you choose to be part of the solution and honor God in showing all His people . . . LOVE?

THE SCHOOLS OF AMERICA

The schools of today are an area of great concern for me. Although, there are many fine teaching facilities across the land, others are equally troubled schools. One of my main concerns is about taking prayer, out of school. I personally feel this is a poor decision and one of the main reasons for the demise, of a quality learning environment. The movement against God has progressed until some cannot even mention God's Name. Many teachers now co-operate with this frame of thinking. Kids are being scolded and punished for talking about God. Some are being silenced at the first mention of His Name. My son was told that there would be "no talk of God" in his teacher's class. You can imagine the effect and humiliation that he felt. I was equally upset. It was clear that my son was living a new and very different reality, than the one that I had known growing up.

The threat of lawsuits seems to be an effective way to hush our people. I have several serious concerns:

The kids have a right to freedom of speech, even if it means God is the subject. Under their rights, the constitution does not "taboo" any topic. As far as I know, every square inch of our country is supposed to be free. Where is it written, that a person surrenders their rights, when they enter a certain building or property. How is it possible that there is prayer on Capital Hill and not in the class rooms of America? Yet, the teachers, students and administrators surrender their rights on school properties. This grieves me greatly. This is a classic example of double standards today in America. The real irony here is that the property belongs to the people of the communities. If it were not for the tax payers, there would be no schools. If you get to the real bottom line "We the people," own America. Our money built the buildings! Why then, do we allow godless people to lord over us and remove our freedom?

The question of the hour becomes, "Is it a wise move to eliminate God from our schools? To help make our decision, a closer look at the teachings of God and His Workings in our nation, is necessary. We would do well to remember, that our nation from the very core, was founded on God. Why should we allow leaders of today, to reverse our Country's most Famous Moments of Freedom? Yet, anywhere in America today, one may find if they look, God may not enter into our public schools. This is a clear violation, of our kid's freedom of speech. Parents are you there and do you care? God's Word teaches one to honor God and people. Love, respect, honor and obedience, are prominent themes of the Bible. Love for all people, even your enemies is a mandate. How would the hallways of America be different, if just these Christian principals were enacted? Love and respect operating in the schools, could counteract most evil mocking. Shootings and suicides might just go down in numbers. Can you imagine a school where children are blest by the Love of God, from their teachers and peers? Taking a look back to the beginning of schools, they were such a place. Today, we have evolved to the heart and mindset of, "no concern to please God." If, we wanted to please Him, we would not have shut the door on Him. To be totally honest, it is hard to respect the message of, "NO GOD IN SCHOOL!" As Americans we know in our hearts, that God is all that is good! If we remove God and all His Goodness and Influence, where does that leave us? What do we have? It is possible to see the principal, that you reap what you sow operating in our schools today? Removing all that is orderly, respectful, good and pure will only result in chaos, hatred and evil appearing. How can anyone respect and honor a system that removes the Highest Calling of our standard? A system that removes God! The spiritual health of our schools may reflect the beginning of the crumbling of our society. Could it be a fore-glance, of a godless society? Remember to take captive our children, is to steal and destroy our nation. Our children are our highest calling and greatest privilege from God. What harm comes to them, when the message of 12 to 16 years is, "NO GOD!"

What about the children, that are not of the Christian Faith. Those who may say today that decent actions of prayer and meeting around the flag pole, would offend them. Well, to them I would extend love and tolerance. I find no loving action in punishing all the children, for the sake of a few. I very much like the old handling of such matters. Families just chose not to participate. It is their right to do so. It is also their freedom of choice. It is a sad day in America and a lost battle, when the masses are punished, for the sake of a few and faith is denied. If the public schools demand that God be banned, then I challenge Christian Americans to rise up. God has given us much wealth. Our top priority should be the spiritual health, of the environment of our children. I challenge our most conscientious believers to build our Christian schools. A place where God's principals can be practiced. A wholesome place, where there is zero tolerance of godless acts. By giving a wholesome environment of love respect and prayer you will be giving our country, a true gift of fine people. To capture a nation, you go after their children. To plant seeds of "Zero tolerance of God," will yield fruit in our future leaders. Likewise to plant Good Seeds of God's Righteousness, will also yield fruit in our future leaders. The truly lost children are those who's parents are not taking the time for church and spiritual matters. For those children their whole world just may be, one without God. There is no thought of God in school and murder and violence by night, from television. In a world where spiritual things are of no concern, who will take the time to counteract, such mental programming? Who among us can really un-do such damage? Such is the plight of many un-churched children. I know that my words are strong, but so are the realities of our days, for our children. We should be concerned about all . . . . of our children! When we take the time to do things right, we will in turn yield a better tomorrow for everyone.

IMPRINTING THE HEARTS
OF OUR CHILDREN

One of my top concerns for this time in which we live, is the hearts and minds of our children. You have heard the old saying, "trash in, trash out!" One absolute truth is that our children are exposed to too much violence, on television. Our news is filled with bad news. Most prime time movies tailor a plot of murder, violence and filthy language.

Night after night, this polluted world, is being dumped into the hearts and minds of our children. When will they receive a cleansing from such degradation? Some music defiles their thinking, as well. How can we expect purity for our children, in the midst of such daily tainting? Yet the call of God on our lives says, James 4:4 "Do you not know that being friends with the world is being God's enemy." 2Corinthians 6: 17-18 commands us, "Come out from among them and be separate, says the Lord. Do not touch what is unclean, and I will receive you. I will be a Father to you and you shall be My sons and daughters, say the Lord Almighty." Americans share a never ending consummation of death, violence, and destruction, in plain view at anytime. Is there any wonder, that there is so much violence and murder on our streets? God describes it this way, "Reaping what You Sow!" Could we actually be stamping the imprint of evil, on the young hearts and minds of our children, instead of the Word of God? If as a nation, we continue to allow moral decay, violence and death to consume our thinking, we should not be surprised by the results we reap. Darkness and chaos could be an unwanted factor in our lives. Are these the elements of murder and violence that is already plaguing our streets? Where are all the great producers that are family and God oriented? Who will rise up and take the lead, fostering quality programming for all ages? Americans seem to be consumed by death, dying and violence on television. Programming needs to be greatly revamped. We should be concentrating on the goodness of life and living well. We should be showing examples of how to love, guide and care for others.

My heart cannot help but wonder, if loving life and living a good life were main stream themes, how might our homes and streets be different? If we reap what we sow, this is one of the most important areas of our lives; the feeding of the heart and minds of our children. Oh, what a quest for service would be rendered by one who wants to make a difference and affect the whole world. Does anyone, really care? If you do, where are you? Rise up, in this world, you are desperately needed!

KEYS TO THE KINGDOM OF GOD

All across America, God has blest this land with young and beautiful new believers in Christ. I pray that God will grant you wisdom, as you grow into a strong young Christian. If you want wisdom beyond your years, it can be found in the Holy Word of God. You will find health for your soul and strength for yours days, when you become a student of the Word! For me, the best type of Bible has been the study Bibles. They contain a wealth of information that you may miss, in a regular Bible. The study Bible will enhance your understanding of the Scripture and keep you growing with new information, long after your expectations cease. You should know that Satan will try to keep you out of God's Word. He will tell you that you don't have time for it. His agenda is always, to kill, steal and destroy. (John 10:10) He wants you to miss out on all the Promises and the Instruction from God that will enable you to stand firm with strength through out your life. If you don't know the Promises, (your inheritance) how can you stand? John 1:1 tells us God is the Word. "In the beginning was the Word, and the Word was with God, and the Word was God!" In John 14: 6 Jesus said, "I am the Way, the Truth and the Life! No one comes to the Father except through Me." Can you see the special relationship with God the Father, Jesus, and The Word. (Spirit of Truth) They are all One, with three distinct Persons! This means that the Word of God, Who is God, is alive with Power! Because it is God! It is the very Revelation of God, to all of His people, for all of time. God has not changed! Hebrews 13:8 "Jesus Christ is the same, yesterday, today and forever!" This is Great News! God's Truth still prevails and He still is in the miracle business! If you buy the lie that you are too busy for the Word, then you will miss out on knowing God, as He desires you to. To buy into that lie, is like tearing down all that God wants to build into your life! There is nothing to be gained, by short changing yourself in the Knowledge of the Living God and His Word! In fact, you may miss more than you will ever know! God gives us another Promise, Isaiah 55:11, "So shall my Word be that goes forth out of my Mouth: it shall not return to Me void. But it shall accomplish that which I please and purpose and it shall prosper in the thing for which I sent it!" One of the most important Truths for you as a new believer, is to understand that true transformation will take place in your heart and mind as you read, understand and apply the Word of God, to your life! In fact, someone said, that you will be, as transformed (like Jesus), only as much as you allow the power and knowledge of the Word, to be alive in your heart and mind! I agree with this in large measure. The other strong working force of God in your heart and mind is His Spirit. It is crucial that, you pursue knowledge of the Person of the Holy Spirit. Which I will be bringing up later.

Many of you may be frustrated in your walk with Christ. Recently, I had the opportunity to talk with some kids from middle and high schools. Our church held a crusade. Some of the young ladies expressed, that they were not receiving a lot from their Christian Life.

Listed here are some of the reasons that could explain the spiritual desert realities of our lives.

1) You can not shelf God and be fulfilled as a Christian.
2) You reap what you sow in your spiritual life.
3) God must be given first place and Lordship, to truly experience Him.
4) Prayer with God is your special time to talk with Him. You can pour out your heart to Him, if you need too. He will listen to you! His Word will comfort you, if you will seek it out in your time of need.
5) Jesus wants to be your best friend, if you will allow Him to be!
6) The Holy Spirit is your own personal God that abides in you. You can not ignore Him and have a fulfilling spiritual life.

The Bible says in Hosea 4:6 "My people are destroyed for lack of knowledge!" Your relationship with God is like any other in your life. You must make a place for Him. If you do not allow the Word, which is God to have a place in your heart and mind, you will not be a fulfilled Christian. The more you devote time for God and His Word, the more you will experience His Presence and Power in your life. To be a successful Christian, you must make a conscientious effort to fellowship and develop your spiritual life thru prayer, and reading God's Word. It is a serious thing to allow Satan to rob us of the time that belongs to God. There are always times in life that are ups and downs. The Word is the ingredient that will anchor you, in the storms. Lordship in Christ means saying "yes" to the spiritual demands in God's Word.

"Yes, I will read my Bible and seek God!"

"Yes, I will pray about everything and thank Him for all He is doing for me!"

"Yes, I will confess my sins to keep open the lines between me and God!"

"Yes, I will fellowship with Jesus in prayer."

"Yes, I will fellowship with other believers at church, which is His Body!"

"Yes, I will obey the commands of His Word!"

"Yes, I will believe in His Promises and accept them by faith!"

"Yes, I will apply His Word to my conduct, decisions and life!"

"Yes, I believe in God's Power in my life!"

"Yes, I will wait on God to answer my prayers!"

"Yes, I accept that sometimes He says no! He knows what is best for me!"

"Yes, I will be faithful to God. He deserves my life!"

"Yes, I will get up, dust myself off and carry on in faith, when I fall down!"

"Yes, I will never give up! I will follow Christ all the days of my life, until I see Him face to face!"

AMEN

JESUS MY BEST FRIEND

Have you ever had a time in your life, when you felt all alone? When you had no one to talk to? I can remember a time, when I felt like this. It seemed like life was hard for me. I am sure that it was in relation to my health problems. The need was great, as it is some times with change and crisis. I found myself on my knees and crying out to Jesus. I remember that I point blank asked Him, "Why don't I have a best friend?" Jesus answered back immediately! He said, "Because I want to be your Best Friend!" His answer to me has been forever burned into my brain! Jesus, is saying the same to you, today! The key is to allow Him that position in your life. The phrase of Lordship, comes to mind. Ignoring Him, and all spiritual things concerning Him, will not get you to where you want/ need to be spiritually.

Did you know that the Holy Spirit is Jesus and the Father, in Spirit form? He comes to live with you, when you ask Jesus into your life. God in Three Persons, the Blessed Trinity! It is important that you ask the Spirit to fill your being and in-power you to live for Him. This is part of the Salvation process. The Bible says that, "We are sealed with the Spirit of God, until the day of our redemption." (Eph 4:30) You could say that He is your Personal Live-in God! Jesus promises to never leave, nor forsake you! His Spirit within us is what makes this possible! The Spirit of God is our Trust Worthy Friend and Guide. One of His jobs is to teach you and enlighten your heart and mind, in the Word and ways of God. (John 14:26) It is important to recognize His Presence in your life. Call on Him, before you enter the Word. He will personally reveal and teach you God's Word! He can be counted on, to always help you to encounter new and hidden meanings and treasures in God's Word. The Spirit can also be counted on to give you strength and power, as you find yourself in need. He is the Third Person of the Trinity of God. It is important to understand and recognize in faith, the workings of the Spirit, in your personal spiritual life. To miss this great revelation is to have a dry and difficult time, when trying to live for God. Revelation and relation with the Spirit, can be the missing factor, for a satisfying Christian life! Always pray about the comings and goings of your daily life. Sometimes, the Spirit will not give you peace about a certain situation, or person in your life. Lack of peace in your heart, can be the Spirit's way of telling you not to continue, in the way you are going. A Sunday School Teacher once told me, "Always follow the peace of God." It is your spiritual barometer, that you are on course for the Lord. (Gal 5:25) The lack of peace over your situation, could very well be God saying to you, "You are going in the wrong direction!" Faith also, is one of the key components for experiencing, God. Faith is a free gift from God. By faith in His Word, prayer and His Spirit leading, you will find the working out of your salvation with God! Satan can try to cripple us, by fear. Fear is the exact opposite of faith. Satan does not want us to experience God's peace and faith. When you operate in faith and peace in the Lord and His Word, you can stand and step out into the world in victory. If you are weak in your faith, ask God for more. He delights in giving His gifts to His children! (James 1:17) The reading of the Word will also build you up in faith! As a Christian stay in these gifts. You will find God and experience His power in your life! True fulfillment with Christ comes with a price. His part was on the Cross. Yours is to co-operate with God, in the spiritual realm. You must realize that investing your time in prayer and the Word is necessary, to obtain a healthy satisfying relationship with God. My challenge to you is simple . . . Sow spiritual things in your life and you will Reap GOD! Remember, that when you neglect your spiritual life, you are missing out on your spiritual purpose in this world for God! (Proverbs 11: 18-19) The HOLY SPIRIT, GOD'S TEMPLE IN YOU!

JESUS KNOWS YOU COMPLETELY!

My favorite Scripture in the Bible is Psalms 139. Its' Words are strong and filled with Truth from God's heart, to ours. It reveals the certain intimacy that God has with His children. God shares with us that He knows us completely! There is One Who is all knowing. He knows you better than you know yourself! The God of the whole universe knows your name and heart completely. I know that such a revelation can be over-whelming. Some people desire to live their lives independent of God. They seem to resent the intrusion to the core, of their inner being. I beg to differ with you, on this very important point. I can only hope, that you can understand and grasp, that the exact opposite is the actual truth. It has been my experience, that God having complete knowledge of me, has brought me reassurance and comfort. You see, with complete knowledge, comes total understanding. I would not want a God, who could not completely know and understand me! The reason for this is a simple one. As God's child, you can rest assured that He knows exactly why you do and say, the things that you do! Such complete heart knowledge, reveals the internal motives of our hearts. God knows all the "why" factors in our lives. For my God to know me better than I know myself, brings me great comfort and trust. Let's just think about this for a while and put it to the test, to find what such knowledge means to each of us personally. He knows all of my circumstances. He knows all of my hurts and pain. He knows exactly, how I got to the point that I am at! He knows when I lash out and why, I did so! He knows my HUMAN SIDE!

The Word says in 1Corinthians 10:13 "No temptation has seized you except that which is common unto man. And God is faithful; he will not allow you to be tempted beyond what you can bear." But when you are tempted, He will also provide a way out so that you can stand up under it." I know in my heart, that since He knows everything about me, He totally understands all of my actions too. That kind of glorious knowledge brings His wonderful grace right into the prime time of my every need. Where ever you find yourself today, whether it is in hurt, failure or pain, there is a God who is totally aware of your every need and He cares for you! He knows every tangle in the web you have weaved. He knows the areas that will certainly snare you. Always remember with His special and complete knowledge of you comes, complete understanding. With complete understanding, you can find mercy and grace for your time of need. With His mercy and grace, God is giving you a new chance at your tomorrow. Tomorrow will come and you will find His love, will never fail or desert you. You have a priceless pardon awaiting you, if you will only come and acknowledge Him. I find comfort in knowing that I don't have to explain to God, why I did or said what I did! He already knows and understands! What a liberating truth is ours in Christ Jesus! You don't have to wrestle with yourself any more! Just let His Grace cover you! Your Father awaits you. He wants to talk with you about your needs. He wants to help you, in your time of great crisis. The choice is yours! God chose you a long time ago, in a very painful and expensive place called Golgotha. Where because of His great Love for you, He rendered His Life to buy and pay for your complete justification. (just as if I had never sinned.) The Glorious Gift of Life is always paid in full. Your part is to find a place in your heart for Him. Then, come willingly and accept His finished work on the Cross for you!

Jesus's work is complete. He lacked giving us no good thing. You only have to accept His offer and open your heart to an Almighty, All Loving God! The next step is a little harder. You must forgive yourself and move on, past all the things that have bound you up! Christ is the Great Liberator of all Life! Psalms 34: 17-18 tells us that not only does God hear us, but will rescue us as well. If you are broken hearted and crushed in spirit, God longs to rescue you. If you will only allow yourself to open up to Him and give Him the problem. Then, you are one step closer to victory. Sometimes, victory can be as simple as being freed from a problem that wants to dictate your life.

Most of us have heard the saying, "let go and let God." Some times that is the simple solution and way of peace, in the midst of a problem. We must take our hands off the ball and put it in the hands, of the Master. From our hands to God's Heart . . . two hearts that trusts each other. Heart to heart with God, surrounded by His capable hands is a place of peace, rest and comfort for the weary. There is no doubt, that God is able . . . WILL YOU COME? You will find rest and peace for your soul!

Matthew 11:28 "Come to Me, all you who are weary and burdened and I will give you rest. Take My Yoke upon you and learn from Me, for I am gentle and humble in heart and you will find rest for your souls. For My Yoke is easy and My Burden is light."

A MANDATE OF LOVE NOT A CHOICE.

As a Christian in America, we are under a Covenant with God. We are saved by the shed blood of the Lamb, Jesus. The One who was born to die and safely deliver our pardon. We are sealed by the Presence of God Almighty, as His Spirit partners with us. Our quest involves learning how to allow God, to live through us. If our lives are to be pleasing to God, we are to be willing, obedient vessels of the Holy Spirit. God has called us from the beginning of time, into fellowship with Him. In the Garden of Eden, one of the most meaningful times He called for Adam and Eve, was after they had sinned. He can be found calling them, unto Himself. This is an eternal spiritual picture, of a God Who seeks and calls His children. Genesis 3: 6-9, shows us that the fall of all of mankind had taken place at the hands of Adam and Eve. God can be found walking in their garden and seeking fellowship with them. What a powerful, wonderful eternal Love is displayed from the heart of God, to His children! The God of the Bible has not changed. His interest in us still remains! The question is . . . . Will you trust His heart and obey? Like Adam and Eve, you may be fighting a battle of great consequences. God can still be found walking in the midst with you and calling you unto Himself. Psalms 18:2 testifies to us about our God. "The Lord is my Rock, my Fortress and my Deliverer; my God is my Rock in Whom I take refuge. He is my Shield and the Horn of my Salvation, my Stronghold." Oh, what gifts, Jesus died to deliver to us. What glories we forfeit, when we fail to give Him our hearts and take His hand!

In return, we are to be His holy people and witnesses. Matthew 28:19 gives us our non-negotiable mandate to "Go and make disciples of all nations, baptizing them in the Name of the Father, and of the Son and of the Holy Spirit, teaching them to obey everything that I have commanded you. And, surely I am with you always, even unto the very end of the age." We are to tell the world about Him. Let Him be our hands and feet. I have often wondered, how many people we will walk by in our lifetime?" Will it be millions that we have encountered and yet, remained silent about Him? Have we seen people in need of Him and not said one word?

Seeing this picture makes me wonder, if we think we are exempt from the task assigned. Apostle Paul, clothed with the Spirit of God, turned the world upside down for Christ. He is the one man accredited, with putting the Gospel on the map. If one man can do such mighty things under the power of God, what can He do with us? Can you even comprehend what could happen, if millions of Americans all over the world suddenly became obedient to the call to go? How would the face of the world change for Christ? I challenge you to re-think your position on the Great Commission. Examine your heart to see if you are walking obedient to the greatest assignment that you will ever be given. God said, the harvest is plentiful, but the workers are few. (Matt. 9:37) As Christians, we are without excuse because we can go. Pray for God's heart and mind, his ears and desires daily. Then, you can be tuned in for the purpose of each day. Perhaps, you are to listen, comfort or show love to someone in need. In doing so, you have served the Lord Himself. (Matthew 10: 40-42)

WHAT IS PRAYER WALKING ANYWAY?

God allowed me to go to the mission field with a sister church. I had always thought that mission work was building, nails, hot sun and hard work. Exhaustion always came to mind. I knew, I could not endure such activity. Therefore, I had not entertained the mission field, seriously. In short, I had a distorted view of mission work. Although, my Dad was a Master Carpenter, you would not want anything I could make. It would be discarded, shortly after birth! Therefore, I was out of the ball game with mission work. However, the day came when I found out that mission work, can be as simple as praying and walking. That's right, if you can pray and walk, you are on the list and requested to come to the mission field! My second obstacle was that I did not understand the concept of prayer walking. I knew that you can pray about anything any where and get the same results, right? So, what is up with prayer walking? But, the fact that it is on a list somewhere, as a requested activity means it is important. I asked the Lord to give me understanding of the benefit of this activity. God heard my prayer and revealed to me, the story of Jericho. We find the instruction to walk seven times around the city of Jericho. We see the people walking in faith obediently around Jericho. The rest is history . . . the walls fell and the battle was won. I found myself wondering, what would have happened if the people had ignored the calling. How many battles of Jericho have passed us by, because we have ignored the call. Battles with certain victory, but we failed to answer, in the Spirit. We handled that battle with the power of the flesh and found defeat and loss. I know you are like me, we want the strongholds to fall and the walls to come down! Right? Prayer walking is about a people of obedient faith, encountering a Supernatural God. It is about a place or problem, that could remain untouched by the power of God, if left alone. Or, it could be compared to a tornado. A place where the Supernatural Power of God touches down, as faith filled people usher in His Power and Glory . . . Where God comes there is glory, transformation and blessing! It could be just an ordinary place, where God chooses to display His signs and wonders.

I have heard it said, that miracles, signs and wonders have ceased, as in the Bible days. I know that God's miracles, signs and wonders have not passed away. How do I know? Because, if it were so it would be recorded in the Word. Instead, our God awaits faith filled people, who truly and obediently believe in His Supernatural Power. The Word says it this way, Hebrews 13:8 "Jesus Christ is the same yesterday, and today and forever." John 14:12 "Most assuredly, I say to you, he who believes in Me, the works that I do he will do also; and greater works than these he will do, because I go to the Father." Oh, if we could only grasp the true Nature of our Almighty God, who waits for us. I am reminded of this Truth, "Seek and ye shall find." Matthew 7:7.

09-11-01

It was about time to get ready for my first mission trip. Our destination was to be Lisbon, Portugal. We were going on a choir tour, to sing, refresh and lift up the missionaries and believers on the field. We had about 30 people prepared and ready to go. Excitement had definitely set in. Then one day the phone began to ring unceasingly. My husband was calling me, to tell me to turn on the television. He said, "An airplane had just hit the twin towers in New York." As I watched in disbelief, I could not fathom what horror we might see. It was then, that my world turned upside down. It seems that anxiety had grasped our whole nation. It was no longer safe to travel or fly. Yet, I was scheduled to go! Of course, my husband and family did not want me to go. One of my best friends and many others, backed out of the trip. The choir became an ensemble, as only about 15 people still wanted to go. My heart told me, that this was a God thing and I was to go on. The pressure of the matter in conflict, made me feel totally torn in two. I struggled with the anxiety that going, would cause my family. But, the Holy Spirit tugged at my heart that I was to still go. I honestly felt incapable of making a decision to go or stay. I cried to the Lord to help me and guide my decision. God heard my cry. He did guide me. In fact, He stepped in!

It seems Air France airlines could not be allowed to enter the country. They could not pass security and be given permission to land. No plane, meant no trip. At least, not until spring 2002. It was neat to see God Himself, step in and make the decision for me. That is the God that I serve and write to you about today. This is one of the ways, that I know and have experienced Him. God is attentive to our prayers. He is able and willing to help us in our times of crisis, if we will open our hearts and lives to Him. Oh, may we encounter Him and the power of His Name, as often as we need Him, or His will has ordained! "For you will light my lamp; The Lord my God will enlighten my darkness. For by you I can run against a troop, by my God I can leap over a wall. As for God, His Way is perfect; the Word of the Lord is proven; He is a Shield to all who trust in Him." Psalm 18: 28-30. Of what then shall we be afraid? Our certain victory awaits us!

OUR FOCUS .... GOD'S TASKS;
FULFILLING GOD'S WILL

As I write this book, I know that there are countless wonderful fellow believers who, really love the Lord Jesus. You are those, who seek and follow Him in service. You would not be found being a back row participant. One who appears and disappears like the wind. To you I say, "Keep on with the good work that the Lord has given you!" My concern here is for the churches that are full of people all around the world that have already missed His target. God has a plan, a reason for being . . . for each church and His people. So many churches today are not realizing their calling from God. One tell tale sign, is a church that is turned totally inward. This focus is always the wrong direction. It leads away from God's purpose and plan. While there is certainly nothing wrong with ministering among your members, this should not be the total focus. The church is always called out. We must come out and be known to the community. The church body should be bearing fruit and doing good works for all the world to see. A church that is turned inward and hides behind its walls, has lost its' direction and purpose. I fear that many people feel that the Great Commission (Matt 28: 18-20) has an exempt clause and they are exempted out of it. After all, we have and support the missionaries on the field! Right? This misconception could be one of the biggest problems of the modern day church. In the book of 1 Peter, God explains the calling that He has placed on the life of every believer. 1Peter 2:9 "But, you are a chosen people, a royal priesthood, a Holy nation a people belonging to God, that you may declare the praises of Him who called you out of the darkness into His Wonderful Light." Jesus is our Spiritual Father, Who shares with us His missions. We are the body that is called to bear witness to the Living, All Powerful, Holy God! (Isaiah 43: 12-13) Just as each of us are related to Him as our Father, we also, have inherited His mission work on earth.

Our primary focus and tasks are to show His love to the world around us and to help them come in salvation, unto Him that saves completely!

Practicing walking in the love of God is a broad task. It covers everything from walking in peace with your brother, to helping the poor. It has many avenues of works that we as a body should be showing forth, to a lost and dying world. The question that comes to mind is this, "Are you in the ball game, or are you in time out?" Are you, the greatest player of all times, or have you given up and just lost the game. It is never too late to be revitalized in our faith. Jesus is the Author and Finisher of our faith. (Hebrews 12:2) He can and will revitalize your heart and mind, to care about His Purposes and Will on earth. Let the God of light shine in your heart and mind to reveal to you, His hidden Purposes. That they may come forth and shine like a diamond, working in the greatest privilege on earth. We are to proclaim His Being . . . . The Great I AM, who completely Saves His people. Do you really believe that you have the answer? If so, you should be shinning brightly and illuminating the path to God!

WALKING WITH GOD MAKES THE WORLD, A BETTER PLACE

We are the body of Jesus Christ and He is the Head of the body. (Romans 12: 5-8) It is vital to our well being that we be in touch with Him. As with any leader, the success comes when we follow the Master's plan. The God given task of soul winning must be abounding in the Spirit's power. Have you ever looked at a day, through His spiritual eyes and ears? If so, you may find that the purpose of your day was a spiritual one. Oh, what a changed world we would have, if we walked our life out, in love for God and others! Perhaps you might visit a friend and find that she begins to pour her heart out to you. Then, the purpose for that day is to listen, console and pray for her needs. Add her to your personal prayer lists. Check on her again. Show her/him, that you really do care and this was not a chance encounter!

Maybe, the next week you run into someone that is ailing. Your purpose for that day could be to listen, reassure and tell her, you will pray for her. The idea is to allow God's will for each day to be your focus. For most Americans, the biggest hindrance to our being on our toes spiritually, is our schedule. Sometimes, I think we need to lay it down, in order to make God's agenda for the day, our primary focus. We can have many things, competing against this kind of mind set. But, if we will begin our day in prayer and put Jesus in charge of everything that concerns us and our families, we will find a better quality of life and a sharper focus on Christ. Another suggestion is that you ask God to quicken your heart and mind, when opportunities to minister knock. Then, when He does, your part is to listen and heed. Participate with Him wholeheartedly, as opportunity arises. For a Christian to be successful in their daily walk, starting the day yielding to God and taking His Spirit is essential for victory. In the spiritual realm, we reap what we sow. If we don't cover our bases, in fellowship and prayer with God, we will find the ballgame a rigorous struggle, with opportunities missed and time out for bad behavior! Either you are covered in mercy, grace and power with readiness of heart and mind, or you are in the battle undressed and free faultering. We could find, there was little attention to anything spiritual, as we address only those things that take priority.

I like the idea that if you come in contact with someone, for more than a minute or two, then it is possible that this is an ordained Divine appointment. Living with this mind set the day will become an adventure. God will hold your hand, leading the way and showing you what needs to be done. It is a fact, that most days can be exciting, as God takes your hand and leads you on an adventure, designed specifically for your day! What a peace enters in, when we put an Almighty God in charge of ourselves, our concerns and our family! God can use everything from our acts of love and service, to kindness of heart and word, to shape the world around us. Many people are in need of their vision refocused back toward God. Can we even imagine a world where Gods' purposes are constantly spoken and attended to on earth? The seeds of which, could easily turn others back in the right direction. At this time in America, it certainly is not a time for us to remain silent! Silence regarding spiritual matters, has never been an option for us. Instead, our constant focus should be willing service directed from God's heart to others in the world around us. We must not listen to the voice that tries to convince us, that such matters are private and of no concern to us. To buy this lie is to knock ourselves out of the ball game completely! I believe that God would always rather we seek His guidance and sow seeds of love and truth to the hearts of others; than show ourselves uncaring and silent. Or, have we simply forgotten one of the main reasons we are here, that is to mirror God, Jesus Christ the Savior, to the world around us. This does not mean that we should run people down with our truth. But as God provides, prompts and affords us the opportunity, we should grab it obediently! Fear is natural, but cannot enter into the equation. Fear can stop you dead in your tracks and limit your usefulness to God. Following Him and yielding in faith has to be our operative plan. Lordship and faith cancels out fear and disappointing God. As we go we walk in faith, yielded and allowing Jesus to minister through us. In the Word, Jesus tells us not to worry about what we should say. Matthew 10:19-20 says, "At that time you will be given what to say. For it will not be you speaking, but the Spirit of your Father speaking through you." As one friend said to me recently, "Just let him out!"

Will you for Christ sake, take a look at the people around you? Those whom our God has placed in your life. Who needs a word of encouragement? Who is headed in the wrong direction? Who is in need of healing, from the God who heals the broken hearted? Isn't it time that we allow ourselves the opportunity to show the world that we care! We as Christians carry the answer to all of life, in our bodies. We are the temple of Gods' Spirit. It is our God given responsibility to impart the love of God, and His truth to the world around us. Only God who goes before and after us to continue the work, knows the full impact of our obedience. With a life focus like this, it is impossible to miss the reason for our being here. Then, we will find the contentment that is rich with spiritual blessings, as we fulfill our God ordained purpose on earth. Psalms 37:23-24 "The steps of a good man are ordered by the Lord. He delights in his way. Though, he falls, he shall not be utterly cast down. For the Lord upholds him with His hand!" Are you walking your journey hand in hand with the Lord? If not, you could be missing out on some of the most important blessings God has in store for you and your family! Oh, what glory and joy fills the heart of a person who will seek and fulfill Gods plan, daily walking it out with Him!

WALK IT OUT BY FAITH

Recently, I had the privilege of going to Venezuela on a mission trip with my church. We had a team of 30 people on mission for Christ. At the time, little did I know, that this trip would be one of the highlights of my Christian life. If you are willing to make the investment to go, you will be blest. God Who is Faithful, allowed me to be a useful vessel for His kingdom. At His prompting, several people were saved. I was amazed to see the anointing of God upon us. Everywhere we went, people were saved. I have never encountered a situation quite like that. When I first made the decision to go, my heart was touched for God's Will to be done. But, it was several months before we actually left the States. By the time it was close to time to go, some doubts had entered my mind. The full assurance that I was to go was mingling with some doubts. The fear of the unknown was mainly what I was feeling. I found that I had to make a choice, on what I would believe about my trip. I chose to lay aside the feelings of doubt and fear. These emotions are not a place that you can park your heart and mind in. If you receive them as your truth or lot in life, they will consume you. However, fleeting these emotions were, they were still present in the playing out of God's Will for me. It was God's Will that I go! As it turned out, an incident happened to me that would prove that I was in the center of God's Will.

As we were returning home on the plane, I found myself trying to give my seat away to some friends, so that they could sit together. Emory said, "No let her sit over there with my son." About this time, I looked up and there was an older gentleman with a cane looking down at me. He explained that he was to sit with me. I did give him my seat, so that he would not have to climb over me, if he needed out. He sat down and began to talk a little with me and then the conversation ended. I began to read my book. It was a long trip home and I was tired. I just wanted to relax and read my book. I began to sense that he wanted to talk with me and that I was supposed to talk with him. To be honest, I really just wanted to be quiet and read. But, I felt convicted to quit being selfish and attend to him. So, I laid my book aside and gave him my full attention. He seemed

41

very much like a man with compassion. His heart was touched that we had been on mission to Venezuela. It turned out that his wife was from there. He told me that he was an agnostic. Of course, this did not sit well with me. He began to explain, that he had heard about Jesus and the God of the Muslims. He said, "There was no doubt that Jesus was the most beautiful person that ever lived." But, he explained, "I am confused about God and have prayed to God for understanding." I answered, "Today is the day that God has chosen, to answer your prayer!" He said, "I have no faith!" "If only I had faith!" I told him, "that the reason that he had no faith was that he was spiritually dead." I explained that, "faith was a gift from God." And that, "when the Holy Spirit comes into him, that he would have a new life and faith." For the rest of the trip home, we talked. I was able by God's grace to answer every question that he had! I began to share that I sort of had this thing, "I want to take as many people with me to heaven, as I can" "I want to take you with me to heaven," I said. I ask him, "to realize that he could not afford to be wrong and that his spiritual destiny was at stake!" "If he did not except Jesus, then he would go to Hell when he died." To which he promptly responded, "The Pope says that there is no Hell!" I quickly answered, "The Bible says that there is." "It is a place of weeping and gashing of teeth." "It would be a permanent situation for you." After that we talked about the Holy Trinity, the Cross and Jesus. He said, "I have met a lot of Christians over the course of my life and they have been exceptional people." (He was beginning to think about Jesus's offer.) It was a fact, that they had modeled Jesus before him. Their seeds were about to bring forth a new kingdom birth, as the Truth sprang to life, in this man's heart!

Our time together was growing towards a close. The plane was soon to land. I could sense that he may not be ready to make a decision. I told him that I would tell him how to accept Christ, so that he would know, when he was ready. I began to share with him in his ear the Sinner's prayer. When I finished, he said, "I am going to do that!" "I am going to do that right now!" It surprised me, but I led him in the prayer. I instructed him to get a Bible and find a church. He confirmed that I was Baptist. He prayed, "Lord Jesus I know that You are God. I know that You died to forgive me of my sins. I ask You to please forgive me now, of all of my sins. Please come into my heart and be my Lord. Fill me with Your Holy Spirit. I want You to be the Lord of my life. I will serve You all the days of my life. Thank you for forgiving me of my sins and saving me. In Jesus name I pray!" AMEN! I congratulated him on his salvation and told him now he had a new life in Christ and faith. I then asked him to, "please go and get your family saved!" He had a wife, six children and four grandchildren. He said that he would. As he started to leave, I said, "Oh, one more thing . . . . I will never see you again on earth but, I will see you in heaven." He asked, "Is it a date?" I said, "Yes!" He began telling people that he had a date with me! By this time my team members were aware that we had yet another person, saved on our trip! They began to hug and congratulate him too! He de-boarded the plane and called for me to come and meet his wife. He promised to share the prayer with her and I felt confident that she would be coming to Christ too! Tears and the words, "Thank you" flowed from him as God's new Life was taking root in his heart. For me, this event confirmed God had not only intended for me to go on that trip but, that He had reserved my seat! It was all in His plan for me to be on the Venezuela team. The truth emergences, that doubts and fears can not be the driver of our life. They will trip you up and cause you to miss out on God's plan for your life. Always remember, that fear is the opposite of faith. God's Word promises us, "that those who trust in the Lord will not be disappointed." Therefore, everything in life becomes a matter to trust Him with. Our God is the God of the Bible. The Bible is written for us to know Who He is. Not, to know Who He was. (Heb. 13:8) "Jesus is the same yesterday, today and forever!" That leaves us with an All Powerful God who is still victorious! My God is and has always been a Supernatural God, Who answers the prayers of His children! For one to expect less of Him, is to miss Him in His fullness and power. There will be times that fear and anxiety will knock at your door. But, these are only opportunities to reflect back on all that God has done for you in the past. Then you can meet the challenge in full assurance that He will provide again. His name is Love, His Heart is willing and His Ear is attentive to your prayer. A wise man will replace fear with faith, in an All Powerful God and keep walking on their journey. Victory is only a prayer of faith away! Resist doubts in faith and you will find strength to continue in your journey.

ONE WAY ONLY TO SALVATION
AND HEAVEN .... JESUS!

The world will tell you that there are many Gods and ways to enter into eternity. "All roads lead to heaven," as I am sure that you have heard. Right? Unfortunately, this expression is a lie. Another popular lie is that, "if you lead a good enough life, you will enter in." A possible third lie that cost people their salvation is, "I will wait till I clean up my life." The problem with these lies is that they could very easily cost you, your only chance at salvation. The God of Heaven has a better way for all of us to walk out our lives, while on earth. I want to address all of you that have refused Jesus, for any other God. I have one reason only .... that you too may come to know Him and abide with us in heaven forever! I don't want any of you, to miss your chance to enter into Heavenly Paradise with Christ! Your good works cannot save you! You will never be good enough, at any time in your life to have true righteousness that results in heaven. All good works that are done apart from Christ are not pleasing unto God. You are either His child or you are not. Christ desires that you would come to Him and become His child. He is your Creator already and He knows what is best for you. He wrote our manual. It is the Bible. It is filled with Truth and the Revelation of God's Own Heart, for mankind to grasp. If you offered your righteousness to God, He would be insulted! Do I have your attention yet? I sure hope so, because YOU maybe just the reason that I was led to write this book!

With these next words, I am dead serious! You can not afford to keep on living like you are. If you refuse to walk the way of Jesus Christ, your decision will lead you to an eternal mistake! A decision, that once you die, can not be reversed! God the Father has made it clear in His Word that the only way to Him, is through His Son Jesus and His death on the Cross. Simply because this was His supreme plan and it cost Him . . . His life! Jesus, God the Father and God the Holy Spirit are three Persons in One. A family member recently ask me, "How can this be?" I know it is because He is God! The mystery of His Being is above total human reasoning and understanding. If we put Him in the box of human logic, we will never see Who He really is. What this means is that Jesus was God in human form. The Almighty God that chose to leave the comforts of a heavenly celestial world, to come to rescues His creation . . . You! In John 5:24 Jesus says, "I tell you the truth, whoever hears my Word and believes Him who sent me has eternal life and will not be condemned; he has crossed over from death to life." God the Father sent God the Son and gave God the Spirit, to all new children/believers of Christ. Jesus supreme reason for coming to earth was to die for your sins and mine. He is the Lamb that was slain before the foundations of the earth were laid. (Rev. 5:9-10) God's plan has always been in existence for us. All that He did, was for you! Jesus died the most cruel death known to man. It was His plan to freely and willingly give His life, so that all of mankind's sin debt could be forgiven. He will certainly give to all who will listen and come, eternal life with Him in heaven. Jesus is the free Gift to all of mankind that cost His life on earth. But, the choice is yours to make. He will not force Himself on anyone. Now, just for a moment, put yourself in the shoes of God. If you have done all of this, just to rescue mankind and bring them into eternal life, would you allow any other way for people to enter into heaven? Being human the answer is easy for us, of course not! Then in the light of this reality, why can false teachers say that they know another way and any of you believe it? God's Supreme Sacrifice cost Him every ounce of His life blood on earth. Any other way would be stealing and cheating. The Lord Jesus says plainly, "I am the Way and the Truth and the Life. No one comes to the Father except through Me." I whole heartedly understand and say Amen! This act of God through the Son, is a once for all deal. No other person, or so called god has done this for us! This is the truth and why all roads do not lead to heaven. Jesus' work on the Cross is finished. The choice to come to Him is a free one. God the Father always calls and desires for the whole world to come to Him, thru the Son. He paid the price for all of our sins. You don't have to earn a pardon. You just have to accept one that has already been given. His Name is Jesus Christ the Lord of All! The death of Jesus calls, "Come, You are forgiven and will inherit eternal life in heaven!"

Remember, however the opposite is also true. Your destiny is of your own making. You can choose to live with Jesus or die in your sins, because you rejected Him. The Bible also plainly says that Hell is a real place. It is a place where there is weeping and gnashing, of teeth. (Mt 8:12) Once, you are there, you will never return. You will live eternally in darkness and the tortures of hell. Remember and consider, the offer was free and you had a choice. If you will, please come now to Jesus and accept His death for all of your sins! Let him lighten your burdens and take the load from your shoulders. His blood will cleanse you white as snow. You will be washed in the blood of the Lamb. Ask Him to forgive you and be the Lord of your life. Thank Him for loving you so much that He gave His life, for you to go free from the penalty of sin. Ask to be filled up with His Spirit. Then start walking a new life through the indwelling of the Holy Spirit. He will walk every step with you and never leave or abandon you! (Mt 28:20) "And surely I am with YOU . . . always, to the very end of the age."

You may not feel any different, but you are. You have transferred sides and are now on God's team. Your journey will be in His hands. You will find many blessing on your life. God will direct your path. His ordained works that you do will be pleasing to Him. His will and desires for your life will flow through you. You have just received the Best Friend that you will ever know! In the Person of the Holy Spirit, He comes to abide with you and seal you as His, until the day of your salvation, or He comes again to receive you unto, Himself. The Holy Spirit will teach you and guide you. You will know true peace and joy that comes from abiding and trusting in Him, who resides in you. The emptiness that existed before He came to you will pass. You will be transformed with God's purposes for your life. Life will have bliss and meaning. Praise God the Father, the One who sent Jesus to rescue you! He is the one, who will close out time and end all of history holding all of life in His hands. My heart for you all, is that you will be counted present on this coming day of Glory! Jesus is truly the only Way for your Salvation! Come now, accept Him and believe. He will come and abide with you forever, showing you the true purpose for your life. Roman 8: 38-39 "nothing can separate us from the love of God that is in Jesus Christ our Lord!"

THE TRAP OF: "I WILL COME TO JESUS WHEN I CLEAN UP"

On my heart today are the millions of Americans, who have heard of Jesus, yet they don't really know Him. The Bible makes it clear that you are either a child of God or a part of the world. You may be one who has head knowledge of Him, but no real personal relationship with Him. You may wish to live your live to the fullest and have no regard for church or anything pertaining to God. Perhaps you find that you are neutral on the subject. You are thinking that you have plenty of time to address God, at some later point in life. If this describes you, please listen to my heart of truth to you. The problem with waiting till the time is right, is nothing short of a lie and a trap of Satan. The Bible describes him as a liar who comes to kill, steal and destroy. (John 10:10) That's right Satan wants you to miss out on your chance to enter into your especially prepared place, in paradise. Jesus said, "In my Father's house there are many mansions, if it were not so I would have told you. I go to prepare a place for you. And if I go to prepare a place for you, I will come again, and receive you unto Myself; that where I am there, you may be also." (John 14: 2-3) Can you see it, a mansion in paradise with Jesus? I want you to think for a moment about the possibility of missing all the glories of heaven because of procrastination. And, that is exactly what has happened to untold millions of people, who thought that they had all the time in the world. Isn't that scary? The worst part is that this could be what will happen to you! Is it worth it? You are choosing a life that for the most part, is designed to not fill the emptiness of your deepest longings. In effect, you have traded away eternal happiness, for the life of this world. Now, think for one more minute about the condition of this world. What are you thinking? It certainly is not worth the tremendous loss that you will be facing! If you are thinking that you would like to wait until a certain age, where accountability is important to you, that is just another trap.

Statistics show that the older you get, the less likely you are to be receptive to the Gospel. It does happen of course, but it is just as likely that it will not happen. One reason for this is that the process of living life can harden your heart toward spiritual things. Jesus will always hold open an invitation to you, but at some point in dealing with you, He may stop drawing you unto Himself. I see Him as sort of like us, after a few "no's" you just quit asking. If you add this to a heart that has been hardened by life, you could easily see how one slips away into the darkness that God warns us about in His Word. I believe, it is not wise at all to wait on such an important issue. Taking life for granted is a dangerous game, with very high stakes. Buying the lie that you will wait until you are good/clean enough to come to God, may cost you everything. It is likely that day may never come! Speaking from a spiritual point of view, it is impossible to please God, when you are lost in sin. Life lived apart from Christ, guarantees failure in the spiritual arena. I say, this not to judge you, but God's Word says, that you are spiritually dead. Sin equals death. Without the spiritual power that comes from abiding in Christ, you do not have the inner power to perform the transformation of one's soul. (2 Cor. 5:17) This working in a person's life is the working of God Himself, through the abiding Holy Spirit. The Spirit of God is your Power Pack and Source of Strength, necessary for righteousness and obedience. (John 15: 5) Without Him, you are not saved and literally doomed to the choices that you have made! I say this to you, to highly encourage you to consider that now is the accepted time for your salvation. (2 Cor. 6:2) Seek ye God, while He may be found! It is possible that you have never heard the truths that I have shared with you. Or, you may feel convicted towards Jesus. God may be calling out to you right now, where ever you find yourself! It is God's desire that you not wait, but come to Him, just as you are. His blood will cleanse you from your sin.

The God of the Universe is just a prayer of repentance and faith away. God shares with us that He is the Author and Finisher of our faith. (Heb. 12:2) You will start your walk at point A. He will accompany you and take you to your destination. Every need, He will provide for you. His Word will not fail. He will finish the work in you that He started. You will never be the same again! God wants to give you peace, joy and blessings. That is the Heart of the Father that you serve. His Spirit will convict you of your sin. Your part is to repent and walk with Him in faith daily. The process at work in you is called Sanctification and it brings holiness and obedience into your being. He will guide you and teach you the true meaning of life though His Word. These are some of the roles of the Holy Spirit in your life. He is your Personal God, Indwelling Partner and new Best Friend! These Truths are why the Bible refers to your having a new life, hidden in Christ. See it this way, if you could attain salvation on your own, Jesus would not have had to come and die for you! I am sure that history has recorded too many people who have waited and found hell and eternal condemnation their eternal reality. God's heart is not that any should perish! He proved that in His death on the Cross that paid for your sins. Heart to heart, I ask you please . . . . follow in the steps that lead to Jesus. If Satan can cause you to put off your spiritual journey long enough, he wins the battle! It will be you that he gains, stealing, killing and destroying, all that was supposed to have been yours, given to you by Jesus. Oh, that we would care and act in obedience, telling the Truth to others. Saving them from their destruction and loss that occurs at their own hands! The fields are white, ready for the harvest. (John 4:35) Pray for workers. Will you show that you care enough to share and bring them into His ever lasting life?

THE GREATEST LEGAL
SYSTEM IN THE WORLD

To all Liberal and Conservative Judges across our land,

I congratulate you, on being apart of the greatest legal system in the world! If I could have any wish from you on behalf of our people, it would be that you would legislate always in righteous values. Judgments that are consistent with our great Heritage of Faith and Freedom. It has been recorded as one of the saddest days in our history, when prayer was taken out of our schools. Surely, you must know, you will bear the responsibility for ruling against God. Some of you have allowed repeat offenders to go free. The end result was harm, misery, or death to another innocent American. It happened here in Knoxville. A repeat alcoholic offender was released. He had a lengthy arrest record. He was allowed to walk free and the next thing you know, we are cleaning up his drunken accident with another deceased precious lady. It happens everywhere in America and on all levels of life. The laws that were designed to protect us fail and harm us over and over, case by case again! A man that has been arrested 13 times is bound to create tragedy, if given the chance. Why is this not a clear picture and hand writing on the wall? I like the idea of three strikes and you are out myself.

Not long ago here, there were two elderly gentlemen attacked by someone on the streets that had ninety offenses. I have to ask, "Is the innocent lives of Americans precious to you?" Then why do you fail to see that apart from an intervention from God, some people are not rehabilitative material?" It is clear that we need to get tougher, realizing the high cost of making such poor decisions. America in general made a terrible mistake by legalizing alcohol. How do I know? Because of the untold millions of innocent people that have died at the hands of the alcoholic drivers. If we as Americans value life, we must never go forward with more illegal substances becoming legal like this trend. Anytime, a society embraces any kind of sin and legalizes it, tragedy and sufferings are unleashed upon innocent victims.

Another factor knocking at our door such as this is the marriage proposal act; where a marriage would be between two consenting adults instead of a man and a woman. I believe that our children would be better suited, in traditional healthy homes of a man and a women. The contrary is confusing and promotes sin as normal. I can also envision the consequences to young children with their peers, in light of the bullying in America today. Do we care about these children? If we do, we will maintain righteous living in our homes before them. Why would we want to visit our children with more burden and hardship, in this time that we live? We have a Righteous God who watches all of us. We also have a Righteous Manual to go by. The Word says that such actions are an abomination to the Lord. (Lev. 18:22-30) The picture is an eternal Truth of right and wrong from the Creator of our lives. When we ignore God's Word and find that we are in breech of it, by our actions, we will bring on certain judgment. These decisions are serious, with serious consequences. The promises of God are true and real, including the ones about judgment. It is a sad day for us, when we find it necessary to deal with such moral matters.

If we follow the wrong road with morals, our homes could fail our churches could fail, and then follows our country. Not to mention the unleashing of sensuality and moral decay, that will be visible to even our youngest! Do we want a country like this? A country that is just a heart beat away from judgment and possible destruction? Is this the legacy that we want to leave our children? And, is this the best world that we can give them? If we can see the fallacy of this way, we must get our homes in order and live in and practice righteousness. Righteousness starts in the home place and follows into the work place. There is no place that the Righteousness of God should not be able to enter. When God prevails with His people, blessings are unleashed on their land. Blessing or curses . . . . the choice is ours . . . . so is the outcome! (Deu. C-28)

THE TRAP OF GREENER GRASS
ON THE OTHER SIDE?

Another common ailment in our society is the big "D" word. D-I-V-O-R-C-E! As a Sunday School teacher, I have spent many years teaching the Bible to all ages in the church. I have experienced a lot of joy in being with different age groups. One of my favorite classes was the elderly class. They seemed to really love me and enjoy our time together. I used to say that, "when I was finished with them, their next stop was heaven." They were the older class in the church. But, of all the joys of teaching I have known, one ranks up there really high. This would be my present class of ladies. I am one of the oldest ladies in the class. We are a mix of single, married and divorced ladies. We have now spent several years together.

Years ago, we were drawn together by our Pastor's wife at that time, Dacia Thomas. The class was so special, that we decided to stay together for life, if possible. Now we are like sisters! Sharing, caring, rejoicing and praying our way through life. There is no way that I can convey the bond that we have together. But, I can say, that our time together is unlike any portion of our lives. The blending of our lives makes for an interesting time in the Lord. I highly suggest, if you are a divorced, widowed, single or just a lonely lady that you go in search of this class at your neighborhood church. Of course know, this kind of bonding takes time, years really. But, the difference it makes in our lives can only be described in one way, Rich! God has allowed us to enrich our lives with His love and kindness. The sisterhood that we feel helps us to face the world as we know it. We are not alone! You should not be either! Ladies, if your marriage has collapsed or even has seen it's best days, seek the fellowship of the church and ladies who care. They will guide and help you through life. Not to mention, the joy of ministering to the needs of others, side by side. Several of our ladies have been divorced. I can remember the conversation of the class about the difference of income. Even tithing was a struggle, as a result of the loss of income. The comparison was made of the amount that would have been given as a couple, to the amount now given as a single woman. It was very clear that a church may feel the negative impact of a divorce. A large amount of divorces could potentially cripple a church of any size. Over the years, I have heard several Pastors say a word about the "happy factor." It is common for a couple to present with the "unhappy syndrome." It has surprised me to hear Pastors take the opposite approach with couples. They have said, "Who said that you would be happy?" Almost as if happiness didn't count and certainly was not a reason for divorce. But, if the truth is told, lack of happiness is one of the major reasons for divorce. Or, lack of fulfillment in the marriage between partners. Comparing ourselves to others with a high imagination of "what happiness they must have," is another trap couples can fall into. Idealizing other people's relationships and comparing can be dangerous. The truth is that no one knows what is happening behind close doors. You could be deceived in your thinking about others. Satan will try, to sell happiness as the "greener grass on the other side of the road." He could be tempting you with your return to freedom and partying. The truth is that freedom and partying gets old when you are alone. Every couple has their share of issues that need attention. Divorce only adds burdens and hardship to relationships, especially when children are involved.

I can remember a time when I was very unhappy. I was raised in church, and shortly after marriage fell out of church. This was the time that I fell for FALSE temptations, that I thought would lead to happiness. You see, we all have chased the happiness bus! It is a common ailment in our earthly living. Joel and I had just bought a new house. I was seven months pregnant. I believe that is why the man signed the contract with us. He felt sorry for me! After we got the house, I felt the emptiness inside of me. I led myself to believe that, it was because the house wasn't finished. It needed to be decorated! So, I set out to do just that! I decorated until I was completely burnt out on buying. That result would last many years! I quit! Still the emptiness loomed. I am not saying I did not enjoy my life. I did! I had a new baby and I was in love with him! He was the apple of my eye. But, deep inside of me, there was no real lasting contentment. Something was missing, in spite of all of the blessings I was experiencing!

One day, I can strongly recall, my spirit hit an all time low! I started making up the bed, and found myself calling out to God. All I could say was, "God help me, I am not happy!" Well, this was the beginning of my experiencing the God that is always one step ahead of me, as an adult! Within a day or two, my neighbor came over to visit me. The reason for the visit was that God had laid a burden on her heart, for the neighbors. She wanted to make sure that we were all saved! I could not believe this! God had come to me thru Judy! She was a precious woman, who loved the Lord. It was as we were talking that I begin to share with her what was going on in my life. As we explored the situation, we both knew that the problem was that I had left the church, thus leaving behind God. It was at this time that I made a decision to go back to church, and I have never left it again. The lesson for me at this time was that the things of this world can not make us happy. Neither can you bank on any person, as being your total fulfillment. This kind of well being is not of this world! Happiness comes from inside you! It is from God. Knowing and having a relationship with Him and serving Him, is the key to fulfillment in this life. Some thirty years later, I am still pursuing Jesus. I can honestly say that I have never been happier. The reason is that I find myself in love with Jesus and experiencing His personal attention in my life. It is a high that is unequal to any other experience on earth. To think that the God of the universe loves me and is interested in me and all my needs, just blows me away! My definition of a miracle is an answered prayer. When you think about who He is and who we are, the fact that He cares enough to hear me and answer my prayers, is almost unreal! But, believe me, I do believe and thank Him every day! In fact, I am totally convinced of His goodness and love. I believe that if we knew everything that He has done for us and saved us from, we would stay on our knees in adoration and love for Him all the time!

We are made in the image and likeness of God. (Gen 1:27) Over the years, I have heard that being made in the image of God, we have a built in God vacuum. We were created by God, for fellowship with Him. If we try to fill the vacuum with anything other than God, we will experience the emptiness of heart and soul that leads to longing for happiness. When we satisfy ourselves in fellowship and love with God, we find contentment at the deepest levels of our being. I believe that this is the truth and have found it to be my personal experience, on my spiritual journey. So many times what happens to us is the result of our own wrong thinking. It seems we can easily, mislead ourselves into false ideas. After all, if we can believe it who is going to tell us that we are wrong? Hopefully, we will learn by our experiences, that our thinking was wrong. The path we took, only led to new and different struggles. Hopefully, as you have experienced the struggle end of things, you will wake up. The lesson can be found and learned at this point, ideally for a life time. Don't forget the lessons that you have learned. No . . . never repeat them. The answers will always be the same! True happiness is not of this world. It is spiritual and comes into your heart by a King, who loves you and calls you unto Himself. Don't hold the bag of emptiness. Exchange it for the life and adventure of walking with a King! Don't walk away from God, to play in another green field. It is of utter importance that we be obedient to God and His Word. He knows what is best for you, He created you!

Our eternal call has always been to do what is right in the eyes of God and not of man. Contrary to what some believe, no one promised that the right path would be easy. The Word says that we are to share in His sufferings that we may also share in His Glory. (1Pet. 4:13) Out of the pit of suffering, we become righteous and refined in our character. One of the greatest glories a Christian can display is to remain faithful in the face of struggles and temptation. The man who takes the easy way out, will never be quite as gifted in character, as he would have, if he had fought the fight with God on his side and won! What amazing battles we see, when God is in charge of the fight! (1Sam. 17:47). As a nation, under God, we must hold what is sacred and guard our families. They are gifts from above. We must answer the call to stand up for what is right by living that way. Our call from God has always been to put Him first. This means obedience to His Word, regardless of the cost. We must learn of Him and serve His likes and dislikes, by obeying Him. It is the only true path of safety that really exists. I want to walk in the safety net of God! Don't you? What greater gift can you give your loved ones! True peace of mind and heart are the by products of a life spent walking hand in hand with Our ALMIGHTY GOD, JESUS. How about you today, are you trading Him away, entangled in sin? Always remember there is a better way for you. Rescued by the God who saves us from our sins! Get free today and find happiness in the true love of the Living God, the One and only Lord Jesus!

THE MATERIALISM TRAP

Have you ever stopped to smell the roses and take inventory of your life? Did you find the answer to, "what matters most in life?" Surely, God and family would be the all time top answer. But, the flood of truth that comes after this can be deceiving. There is no doubt that we are a very blest nation. But, we must be careful what we allow to influence, our lives. So many messages are paraded in front of us, claiming to show us, a better way to live. While it is true that money is basic for living, the never ending want, of money and things, can certainly entrap us and our families. Happiness, like money, does not grown on trees. One of the leading causes of discord in the home can be linked to finances and money problems. Materialism can grasp a hold on our being and try to define us as "Who's Who," based on material possessions.

The "poor little rich girl" is a syndrome that I have observed in young couples. They go for the status of the big home and fancy cars. Only, to find that their lives are totally restricted due to lack of money flow. I have seen the big house with hardly any furniture, due to lack of money flow. One might find even entertainment, and going out to eat is severely restricted. It is possible to achieve status, by having robbed yourself of an abundant quality of life! As a result, stress disappointment and discord can set in. The problem is not easily correctable, because of the manner of living that has been chosen. I think it is safe to say, that "status living" can be a trap that causes some families to "pay forth their whole quality of life!" Such stern consequences can make this life style unacceptable. I must ask you . . . "What material possessions on earth are worth trading your quality of life for?" It can certainly be a trap that can consume and spoil the plan of God for your life! God wants you to find the joy of serving Him and be rich in family and love. To pursue materialism as a goal to achieve happiness can leave one, disappointed, broke and alone. We are made in the image of God; therefore our happiness lies in the spiritual realm and in knowing Him. Poor substitutions simply cannot bring us to the point of reaching and filling our deepest needs and desires. If one is not careful, we might find our own worst enemy in ourselves!

Sometimes we just need to stop and introspect, who we are and how we got there. The buying of false ideas, can certainly lead us on a trip that we never desired to take! Jesus said it this way, "Build your house on the Rock and it will stand. Build your house on the sand and it will surely fall!" (Matt: 7: 24-26) If we are to know abiding joy and satisfaction in this life, we will do well to follow our Master Instructor, Who knows and will show us the way. "But, seek ye first the kingdom of God and His righteousness, and all these things shall be added to you!" Is it possible that God is telling us that the door that leads to where we need to go to find our true peace and purpose, begins with the aligning up of our souls with Him? Oh, that we would not seek everything that is vain, and leave the most important part of life . . . . our souls . . . unattended! What paths of promise and joy we will miss, if we do!

THE TRAP OF EVOLUTION;
WHO STOPPED IT?

It saddens my heart that our schools teach the theory of evolution. What makes this worse, is the banning of teaching about God. It causes me to think about the innocence of our children. Their heart is to trust teachers and people in authority over them. Like adults, they too are seekers of truth. Lies planted at early stages of development can live for a lifetime. A young heart that has been captured and confused by lies, may never be able to accept, seek or find the Truth. The injustice that was done, could steal a young persons soul!

I had the opportunity to have lunch with a co-worker. She explained to me that she was originally from Ohio. Her belief system stemmed from the knowledge of the classroom, in school. She continue to explain that, "Once she was a Roman Catholic, but, she had denounced her faith." She continued to explain to me, "The schools in Ohio, were so far advanced from the ones, in Tennessee." This experience was the pretext of her current belief in evolution. She stated, "That we are always evolving as a people." I found this statement true, when interpreted in the light of technological advances. However, as I sat across from her, I was totally blown away and speechless. I think I even got choked a bit. It seemed that the knowledge given to her by the schools left no room for the acceptance of the Truth in her life. I could hardly believe that she had actually replaced her God given faith with a lie. I just had to ask, "Who had given her this information that had shaped her in this fashion?" To that question, she replied, "The textbooks in school in Ohio." I don't remember much else about our conversation as I was in shock. Here was someone who thought herself advanced in learning, and was held captive in lies, at the same time! However, she knew where I stood and that was the reason for the conversation. I wonder, if it is really possible for us to measure the damage that is caused by teaching the theory of evolution.

The truth is easy to find, when looking at the facts. Either this theory is true or it is false. I believe that it is a false teaching. One of the best reasons I have for this is very simple. If evolution were a true reality on earth, the process would still be going on. Monkeys would still be turning into men before our eyes. Species would start out one way and evolve into another species, as the process would flow. If the process is one of truth, my heart has to ask, "Then who is it, that stopped it?" However, none of us have witnessed this process today. No man has come from a monkey in my lifetime! If one is inclined to search for truth, the process that is still going forward is the reality of the Person Jesus. He is the most written about Person in the history of the world. The Truth found here is the transformation of ones heart and mind, as life springs forth from being introduced to God Almighty Jesus. The impact of a life with Jesus is a reality readily seen by most Christians. This is a process that is still on going and seen! This is our constant reminder that the only Truth, Life and Way is found in Jesus alone. Christians have all witnessed, transformation, miracles, and answers to prayer. We can testify that God alone holds the creation that belongs to Him. I guess that it is ok to denounce a religion, because none is perfect here on earth. But, one must be really careful not to denounce a Saving Savior, who holds the key to your soul and eternal life! What a privilege is ours in a Savior, Who lived, died and rose again to life ever lasting! (John 10:17-18) Jesus, Who gladly sits at the right hand of God and intercedes for us. (Rom. 8:34) He chooses to hear and answer our prayers. He did all of this because of His almighty love for us. Then one day, our hope will be revealed in Him, as we stand face to face. We will see Him, in His glory!

Oh, what a glorious hope, He holds out to the whole world, with all that He has done. My prayer is that everyone will come and know the Truth. And that you will be able to throw off all the lies, each and every one. The invitation is for all to come to the Christ and be reborn in the Son, Jesus. May we all be present and accounted for, on the day that God the Father chooses to reveal His Son in His Second Coming! (Mat. 26:64)

LIVING THE LIFE OF
SERVICE ON MISSION

Have you ever thought about going to the mission field? Did a tiny little part of you Answer, "No!" You simply can not see yourself there? Well, you are not alone. I am sure that many wonderful Christians, have dropped the idea of mission work for a variety of well meaning reasons. I have spent many years with the misconception that mission work is building. My exposure to the idea of missions was very limited and warped. In my mind, this is how a day on the field went . . . . hot heat, long days and exhaustion. The next day, you get up at the crack of dawn and start again. By the end of the week, you're in a heap and just about dead from the strain! Little did I know, this was a badly distorted lie. It simply is not how it is, in every circumstance on the field. When God called me to missions the first time, I realized how wrong this perception was. If you can walk and pray, you are on a list and needed somewhere to go! Missions can be just that simple! If you can play games and do crafts with children, you are needed! Everyone can participate in missions. Prayer is the biggest need of all and the most powerful service one can render.

God called me to go to Portugal, where He showed me that millions of people are dieing, every year without Christ. Confusion about, "Exactly what is the Truth," keeps millions of people from discovering the One True God. As one bitter young shop keeper almost shouted to me, "Your Jesus has done nothing for me!" Obviously, until my arrival, no one had taken the time to tell her and she could be easily found! She was a young shop keeper in the middle of a thriving trade center. No doubt, thousands of people had passed her by, without one word about Jesus and her need for salvation. I continued to tell her about the death of Jesus, for all of her sins. To which she honestly replied, "Her country has heard from the east and the west." She then explained that many people didn't know who was telling the Truth! Almost everyone that I talked to explained, that most of the church attendance was primarily the elderly. The young generation, did not seem to be interested. Every person that I talked to, with the exception of two, were not saved. It seemed as though the spiritual realm of life there, had been discarded. Before I left the country, God had laid it on my heart to take tracts with me. While I was there, He then provided all of the opportunities to give them away. Each person that God provided seemed to have an air of embracing the Truth. Each took the message and immediately began to read. Most seemed thankful that I gave them the information. While seeing the spiritual climate and need around me, God began to speak a response to them, in my heart. I will reveal this to you. Maybe there will be a time, when you can use this, too. It was simply this . . . . "We have traveled thousands of miles, for you to hear the Truth. Please don't die in your sins. You don't have to. God sent His Son, so that you would not have to perish." Now the message is clear and I am at home. You may have traveled thousands of miles, instead of me. Perhaps our God has brought you right to this point, just to hear about His Son, Jesus. If you have questions about your salvation or would like to be saved then read on. The next Chapter is the Truth, extended from God, for all of the world to embrace. May God's Spirit testify to you, that this is the Truth and it is for YOU!

GOD'S SON . . . JESUS . . . HIS ANSWER TO ALL OF CREATION

"For God so loved the world that He gave His One and Only Begotten Son, that who so ever believes in Him, shall not perish, but have eternal life." (John 3:16.) This verse of the Bible is the most famous verse, of all times. It is the pivotal reason for all of the Scripture Writings. They pointed to the time, when God would reveal the answer for all people of all nations, to be able to find Him and have peace with Him. Jesus' death on the Cross was for all people, both good and bad. Although even good moral people, can not enter into eternity with God, apart from Christ. Their goodness is simply not good enough. The Bible says it this way, "All our righteous acts are like filthy rags." (Isa. 64:6) It was God's brilliant plan to save all of creation through the death of Jesus, His Son on the Cross. Through His death, the debt for our sin has been paid in full and forgiven. One simply has to come to Jesus in repentance and faith, to receive the free gift, He died to give to each of us. Repentance means to express sorrow for sin and turn away from it. Faith is an attitude of the heart and mind that simply says to God, "I believe that You are God and that You died to save me from my sins." God is faithful to His Word and His Covenant. Just as in Bible times, when Jesus walked on the earth, He had to open the minds of His disciples to the Truths of God. My prayer is that with the help of Jesus right now, you too will grasp, understand and receive the special Truths given to each of us in Scripture. Stop right now, and ask God to fill you with His Spirit and give you understanding to what the Word testifies to us, regarding the Godhead.

One Truth that is essential for you to understand is that there is a Godhead and they are Three in One. Jesus said it this way, "I and the Father are one." (John 10:30) There is a Heavenly Father and there is a Son, Jesus. There is a Comforter and His name is the Holy Spirit. The Three are Three in One. You might say three different expressions of God. A family member recently asked me how this could be? My answer to her is this, "That is why His name is God." Just because it seems hard to comprehend doesn't mean it isn't true. Our understanding of who He is, tells us that we are the ones He created. Jesus was fully man and fully God. He had both a human nature and a Divine nature. His birth originated with the Virgin Mary and God the Father. Although Jesus had dual natures, He was sinless and perfect in His life. To understand Jesus, you must realize He was God in the flesh. Jesus, (God the Father), came to earth to save all of mankind. He was to be the sin offering, so that we could be spared and live with Him eternally in heaven. I can remember the day that I understood the Trinity. I was blown away to realize that God the Father loved me so much, that He left the glories of His heavenly home to come to earth, just to rescue me! You and I and our relationship to Him, are exactly what the business of God is all about. The Bible says it this way . . . "He was the Lamb of God that was slain before the foundations of the earth." (Rev. 13:8) Jesus's blood flows from the throne of Calvary. His blood brings new life, as He takes up residence in your heart. Once you were dead in sin, but now you are alive in your spirit, through the indwelling Spirit of God. The Holy Spirit of God comes into the heart of the new believer and seals him for God, until the day that Christ will come again. (Eph 1:13) The Seal of God in the believer's life is eternal and can not be broken. The work of God in our salvation is one of victory. The scripture says it this way, "I give them eternal life and they shall not perish; no one can snatch them out of My hands." (Jn. 10:28) Satan may tempt you and cause you to fall and sin. But, he is powerless to take away your salvation. Supreme loneliness comes when a person, chooses to live life apart from Christ. Many people without understanding are trying to fill the void in their lives, with the things of this world. For them, emptiness of spirit can become a disease. God's place in our lives can never be successfully substituted for things on earth. The Spirit's void in the human heart is a special place that belongs to God alone. Deliverance from emptiness, and meaninglessness of life can only truly be found, when God arrives in the heart of a new believer! When the Spirit of God is allowed residence in our hearts, the transforming work of the indwelling Divine Spirit begins. Although the process is in the beginning stages, it is a life long spiritual quest. God's presence in our lives brings with it new and meaningful reasons for life. Emptiness is transformed into love for God and others. Uncharted paths that belong to God open up, before your eyes. Your life will yield His Ways and Desires. Peace, happiness and blessings belong to the Child of God, who truly keeps their eyes on Him. (Isa. 26:3)

If God has brought you to this very page of this book tonight and you realize that you, need God, please know that I am rejoicing over you with God. His purpose for this book, could be just for your salvation. If you would just bow your head before Him and pray this simple prayer of salvation. This prayer in similar form has been the way that millions of people that have found the Lord Jesus Christ. Pray with me now and know that He hears you, without a doubt!

Lord Jesus, I understand that You are God. I understand that You came to earth to save me, and to forgive me for my sins. I know that I have sinned against You. I am sorry, for all my sins. Please forgive me now and come into my heart to be my Lord and Savior. Thank you for Your precious death on the Cross. Thank you for my salvation. Fill me with Your Holy Spirit and lead me in your pathways all the days of my life. In Jesus name I pray and Thank You! Amen!

My friend the earth may not tremble beneath your feet, but there will be rejoicing in heaven, over your spiritual birth in Jesus! (Luke 15: 7) You have been born again! You need to tell someone. Let the joy flow! You need to find a church and a Bible that you can understand. I like the NIV translation. Find that group of people that love the Lord and will be your life long friends. It is the God given family, filled with Christ love that He longs for you to have! Pray, ask the Spirit of God to teach you understanding of His Word. He will be glad too. He is the third Person of the Trinity and that is just one of His jobs for you! Keep your heart and mind clear and free from sin by confessing your sins daily. You can keep the lines to God clear and flowing to you with power. The Blood of Jesus will cover you all the days of your life. He will be your Personal Life Partner and has promised never to leave or abandon you. Rejoice, your future is secure! He holds you in His victorious hand. Never give up. Never turn away. If you fall, get up, dust yourself off and continue to learn how to walk with God. Just like a new calf, He will strengthen your footing and His Roots will grow deep in your heart. You will find, over time, your life mirrors Him! Shine the Light in the mirror for the whole world to see!

THE TRAP OF: "YOU DON'T HAVE TIME FOR THE WORD."

With the exclusion of Jesus, there is almost nothing as important to the Christian, as the Word of God. To study the Word and have understanding of the Truth will have a profound effect on the student. One of my favorite Scriptures in the Bible is John 1:1, "In the beginning was the Word, and the Word was with God, and the Word was God." The profound truth here is that God is the Word. To know God and His Heart is to know His Word. We are instructed to meditate day and night on His Word. (Jos. 1:8) We are told to hide It in our hearts that we may not sin against God. (Prov. 22:8) He commands us to listen to His instructions. (Prov. 8:33) If asked, a Christian will gladly tell you that one of the most important aspects of their life is their faith. Yet, that same person could just as easily confess, that taking time to get into the Word is a struggle. The pressures of this life, can easily crowd out the Call of God to fellowship with Him. Satan will try to make us believe, that we don't have time for the Word. If we are not very careful, we will find that we have time for everything else, but God and His Word! Yes my friends, listening to that voice can easily result in one of our greatest spirituals disasters. Recently, I heard a speaker say, that you are either growing in your faith or dying spiritually. If indeed, God is the Word, proving true knowledge of Him cannot be separate from the Word. To put it another way, to truly know God is to know the Word. The Word of God is His heart and written Revelation to mankind. Because Jesus and the Word are One, the Word is alive with power, as God is alive on high! Satan knows that our spiritual strength lies in the Word of God. To keep a Christian out of the Word is to retard his growth in the things of God. In a great time of need, one who does not know the Promises of God could lack strength to continue.

Our call is to finish the race that is set before us. Folding is not an option. But, without true spiritual knowledge of the Word, we will never become all that God has intended for us. The Promises of God are true and our True God will be faithful to them. God proclaims to us a wonderful

65

Promise, "So is my word that goes out from My mouth, it will not return to Me empty (void), but will accomplish what I desire and achieve the purpose for which I sent it." (Isa. 55:11) Friends, that is huge! We ought to be reading the Word with our husbands, children, co-workers, friends, lost friends and hurting friends. You get the idea! I believe that God wants His body to impart the Word and bless the hearers! When was the last time that you ask God, for a Word for someone in need? We are only as transformed in our hearts and minds, as much as we allow the Word to renew and change us. "Be ye, transformed by the renewing of your mind." (Rom. 12:2) Without a constant diet of the Word, our inner man/spirit is weakened. Is it possible that some children of God have decided to live in their weakened state and thus, close the Bible and stop their oral witness for God? My friends, if that describes you, your on the down low, with a constant foe who is one up on you and you could lose out on the Master's plan, for your life. Who could perish if you bungle the game or just foul out for a while? Lives are riding, on your choices. One of the true purposes for your life on earth could be hanging in the balance. Maybe God has chosen to use you, to bring home a friend. But, if you are too busy and foul out, anything is up for grabs. One thing is for certain, our God has called His children to be faithful, to all He has commanded. Only the Author Of Our Faith knows our next assignment, and if we have qualified ourselves for the game. Is it possible that by this one choice, we are allowing ourselves to become more like the world, than our beloved God? There is something more sinister going on, when we are listening to the wrong voices and believing it. Without the proper instruction, how can our lives truly be pleasing to God? God's Word tells us, to hear and not obey, is to be deceived. (James 1:22) A person who's life is kept in the knowledge and obedience of the Word matches up with God's heart for Him. That man will be aligned for God's flow of blessings. (James 1:25)

My friends, God has placed an eternal call on all people to know Him, thru His Word. Are you a diligent student in the class room of God? If you are saved, you have already been assigned the Master Teacher. The third Person of the Trinity is the Holy Spirit, who entered in, when you called on Jesus for salvation. One of His roles in your life is that of the "Teacher/ Illuminator" of the Scripture. (John 14:26) Daily visit the throne of grace and go under the fountain of the blood of Jesus. Confessing your sins, you will find He is Faithful and will cleanse you from all unrighteous. (1John 1:9) Then proceed to ask for the Great Teacher to bring understanding of the Scriptures. Jesus promised and He will gladly fulfill the teachable heart. Some of the greatest joys in my life, where found in the time spent alone with God, where He revealed new and profound truths/promises in His Word!

I have a wonderful friend named Liz. We went to church together many years ago. She faithfully, attended Sunday school. On one occasion, she confessed that she could not understand the Word. I was simply puzzled at that! I knew her to be faithful in her attendance to church. It was years after this, that I would run into her again, and she explained that she had found out, that she was not saved! It was simply amazing to hear her talk about the things of God, since the Holy Spirit entered in with salvation! A heart that submits to the guidance of the Holy Spirit will reap enlightenment of the Word, thus fulfilling one of His roles in our spiritual growth.

Don't try to go it alone. True understanding of the Word, belongs to God and is imparted by Him. A prepared believer is one that will be found in submission to the Spirit of God and His daily power for their walk together! The journey will be absent the flavor and power without Him! The Spirit of God is another Partner Of Our Faith that imparts oneness with God. The longing of God's Heart is to impart the treasure of, oneness with Him. (John 15:5) The Word of God is the written inheritance of every believer. But, some children of God never pick up the will, to receive all the treasure that Almighty God has already given to them. To partake in the treasures of the Holy Spirit of the Lord, is to share a walk that is totally unique in Him. Thus finding our purpose; as we daily go hand in hand abiding in Him. My challenge to each believer is to know the joys that have been set before you. Be partakers of the spiritual things of God, in this world. Let God infuse your being with His holiness, through your obedience to His Spirit and Word.

EXPOSING THE TRAP, "SAVED TO SIT"

Friends, have you ever been to the point in your Christian walk that it seemed like you were walking backwards or just plain drying up? The idea of joy is a great but a fleeting one at best! At some point in our lives, we all go through these feelings. Life and responsibilities just have a way of becoming exhausting and overwhelming, at times. Thank goodness that our God understands even our every mood. But, more than this, He knows exactly how we arrived at the point we are at. He is totally aware of every hurt, pain, disappointment and unkindness we have suffered. "How do you know that", you ask? Because the Bible also says that, Jesus walks every step that you take with you! (Ex 13:21-22)

Did you also, know that the Bible states, He knows every word on our tongue, before we speak it? This means, that He also hears everything we say and knows our every thought/intention. Yet, while we were yet sinners, (looking in the total opposite way), He died to save us! (Romans 5:7-8) God's love for us can not be defined or measured. It is simply too large. Our closest comparison is the love of a mother to her child. Yet that is also an inadequate measure. I have tried to comprehend the depth of His love and found that it does help, to compare it to the love I have for my children. While at the same time, realizing that God's love is a Supernatural Love, that trumps any love that can be found on the earth. I hope that you will feel the power of His unfailing love in your life. Then, I pray that you will take the time to shine the Light of His Love into others hearts. When we do, that love will transform and lead them towards our God. The love of our God is so amazing. It begs the question, "What can we do in return?" We can express devotion to God in many ways. One of the most important ways is to serve Him. Service for God can be as simple as, serving a cup of cold water, in His name. (Mat.10:42) Or, it can be as complicated as helping a friend to face an unknown future with sickness and disease. The key is to prayerfully surrender all our ways to Him. Start your day in prayer, even if it is as you are leaving the driveway. Ask Him to fill you up anew and use you to bring Him glory. A surrendered and open heart, our Lord will not overlook. Availability, meekness of heart and surrendering in faith are the qualities that He scans the earth looking for. (Ps. 51:17) This person, God will uphold and use for His Glory. You see, it is impossible for you to know what the day holds. So, in some ways you will never be prepared for the day. But, when we walk hand in hand with a Supernatural God, Who is all knowing, then we are fully covered. It is His power in us that will flow and reach out to touch the world around us. This is His desire. Walking hand in hand with God daily, can be an adventure as we are able to trust in Him. I like to say, "Just let Him out!" Let Him live through you, love through you and save others by His Great Power at work in you. Joy comes when we trustfully walk with God letting Him live through us, touching the world around us.

The Bible says, that God is so dependable in His work in us, that we are not even to worry about what to say! He will speak through us! (Mat 10:19-20) How can this be? When a willing heart in faith, surrenders . . . . God moves through them to touch their world and make a difference! This call of God is eternal. God has chosen to use His people to be His Hands and Feet on earth, while He accompanies and ministers through them. The book of Romans, Chapter eight, talks about such a miracle of faith. We are called, to put off the old man, (by faith) and be clothed in the Spirit of God. Being in fellowship with the Spirit of God, will lead to our lives being used, in His Service in our midst! In fact, God says that it is our spiritual obligation to Him. I agree! After all He has done, it is the least that a grateful child can do. Joy comes, when we allow our lives to be in constant fellowship and service to God. If you are a Christian and you have allowed your life to be totally consumed by this world, you may not know spiritual joy. Joy comes on the morning that you surrender to God your body, heart and mind for His Purposes and Glory, where ever the day may take you. Remember, God is the One who is leading! If we allow ourselves to be saved and sit, then we have forfeited our greatest chance for joy and purpose on earth in God's kingdom!

LISTEN AND HEED

In the times that we live in, it seems like Americans are busier than ever. If we are not careful, the distractions of this life can block out our effectiveness, in the world around us. This could be as simple as the voice that says, "You don't have time right now." Or, the thinking that says, "What is wrong with waiting until tomorrow?" Waiting can prove to be an eternal loss of opportunity. I want to share with you a story of such that happened to me.

In my teen years, I had a very outgoing friend that I ran around with for a while. She lived near Broadway, which is a very busy main street in our town. One night, we decided to go to the Village Inn, for pizza on Broadway. As we were walking, it became dusky dark. Living where she did, she was more experienced at crossing traffic, than I was. As we attempted to cross the street, I was looking at the traffic at a distance out. I started to cross the street. She was looking at the same traffic, only up close. She saw the car that was coming and I did not. My foot went out to start crossing. She simply put her arm out across my chest to prevent me from stepping out. As I put my foot back, I saw the wheels of the car that would have hit me. It would have been a fatal error on my part. I was saved that night from certain death. A favor that years later, I would not return.

As normal, time passed and we went in separate and different directions. She got married and had a child. Her life however, was a troubled and rocky one. Many years later, I ran into her at a store. I watched her from a distance with her child. She seemed her usual outgoing, fun loving self. As I stood there, it tugged at my heart to approach her. But, since so much time had passed, I found myself uncomfortable with the idea of making my presence known. I started making excuses for why I should not follow my heart. It came to me to ask her to come home and talk with me for a while. I felt that I needed to check on her salvation. Feeling torn, I choose to listen to all the excuses, of why I had to pass on the opportunity.

It was a few weeks later, while starting in to church, I would hear the news about her. I was informed that she was partying at the lake with friends, when she had an accident. She was jumping into the water and misjudged the distance. She fell to her death on the rocks below. As the news was trumpeted to me across the parking lot, I felt like someone had instantly kicked me in the stomach. I knew then, "the why" of what I had felt led to do. I understood that day, the importance of heeding opportunities that only come once in a lifetime. The horror of what happened to her was personal to me. I find even today, I have never been able to reconcile the facts about her.

I have wondered, if God used someone else, when I refused to listen to Him. In my heart of hearts, I hoped He did. I wonder if her blood is on my hands. A simple gesture of an outstretched arm, saved my life. When my time came to outstretch the Savior's arm to her, I did not return the favor. I am haunted by my decision, about her eternal destination. I wonder what God will say to me, when I stand before him one day. My hope in sharing this story with you, is that we all would realized the importance of our obeying God. God knew her need and wanted to use me. He also knew what decisions she was going to make, and the hour of her certain death! I challenge all of us, to listen when God tugs at our hearts. Events like this may never happen to you, but God may have something else for you to do, that is just as important! The influence of God speaking through you can be life altering for another person. I wonder, if my friend had come home to be with me to talk, and had accepted Christ . . . . would she still be alive today? She may have found a new life in Christ and passed on her old ways of living.

Sometimes in the natural, what the Spirit of God asked seems unusual. But, it just might be one of the most important decisions you make, when you follow His promptings. Maybe God wants to use you to radically deliver a person and their family from destruction, hardship or death; since His ways are not like ours and His purposes on earth are much higher. You can be sure that He is looking for His children who will rise up in obedience and trust Him. (Isa. 55:8-9) One that will be faithful at a crucial hour in someone else's life. May that person be you! Follow His promptings and let another live to see God eternally in Glory!

GOD GIVES A PERFECT DAY

Today as I sit praying and writing I am outside, by the pool. My sport is swimming. I have been swimming all of my life. It is the most perfect day for it that I have seen, in a long time. The sky has turned from a turquoise to a deep peacock blue. The clouds are big, white and fluffy. The temperature is the perfect "hot" for the water. The water is the perfect cool for swimming. As I sun, my heart is set on praise. I am thanking God for this special day! I sense His Presence with me, as if all of this is a special gift from Him, just to me. In my heart, I give thanks for His perfection. The more I thank Him, the more joy fills my heart. I feel as though, I am swelling with joy. Or, you could say swimming in joy!

This day is a reminder to all of us, that every day is a perfect gift from God; even when our circumstances don't match up. God has something for us to experience with Him, on a daily basis. If you are having a dry spell spiritually with God, this is not His will for your life. Is it possible, that you have missed your time with Him? Are you so busy living life, that your well has run dry? Christians cannot experience the joy that God so desires for us, if we choose to make no time for Him. Palms 1:2-3 tells us how to enjoy our living God. We need to set our hearts and minds to delight in Him and what He wants for our lives. Verse three delivers the promise of the well watered soul, as we plant ourselves in "His river banks."

Many are the seasons of our lives. The times that we enjoy activities and events that may never return to us. Such as the times at the ball field, with little league or the school activities, of your children. All of these things are here today and gone tomorrow, as the pages of our lives are fulfilled and lived out. In comparison, God's plan for us is quite different. He promises us an Eternal Truth, when we are "planted by the rivers of water, that brings forth its fruit in its season, whose leaf also shall not wither and whatever He does shall prosper." Choosing to spend our life in His Presence, we will never be found lacking. To the contrary, He asks us to open our mouth, so that He can fill it up with all the good things He has for us. (Ps: 81:10) Do you need to be watered spiritually? Does you life display the fruit of the world or of God. Many times, the fruit of our lives can be measured by the investment of our time and where we spent it. If you are weary spiritually, come to the rivers of water and plant yourself in His river bank. He waits for you there. His heart is to strengthen you and keep you producing a Harvest of Fruit in your soul. The truly wise, will come to Him confessing and find Him faithful. God says it this way, "you reap what you sow" (Gal. 6: 7-10). What does it mean to be planted in God's soil? It is to have roots that are deep in His soil and drinking in rivers of water flowing from Him. You are entrenched right beside the True Source of Refreshment. You are continually receiving from His never ending supply. Christ made reference to Himself as the Living Water, and said if a person would accept it, He would never thirst again. (John 4:14) The soil of God is His Word. The Word feeds your soul and prepares you to be successful in life. If we are to ever truly mirror our Father's Image, we must have a diet rich in His Word. Just as the body is weak without the proper nutrition, so the soul is withered without a steady diet of His rich soil in our lives!

ADDICTED TO THE WRONG VOICES ... FAILURE OR FREEDOM

When we move through our lives, there will be times that we feel alone. This can be a time, when we are tempted to believe that no one cares for us. In general our society is moving more and more quickly. There is always something in need of our attention. The lists can be endless and overwhelming. If we are not careful, we will find ourselves torn in two different directions competing for our time. Very often one will say, "There is not enough of me to go around." If this goes on long enough and is left unchecked, depression can move in. When we have too much on our plates, sometimes we will fail. Human nature is to cover up failure with denial. You may find yourself making excuses for your failures. Often, one may disengage mentally in the process of facing failures. If we are not careful, we can spin into rationalization and failure. The state of never ending busy, can lead a person right down this path into struggle. One thing that I have realized over the years of my struggle is that, "we are one with our world." Even with all of our denials and rationalizations we can find feelings of failure and depression. Why is it so hard to get rid of this state of being? As long as we are consciously aware of our situations we have to deal with it, in some way. The fact that it is in our mind somewhere in it's recesses, means that you have to deal with it, one way or another. Many people play ostrich and pretend to ignore problems, as a way out. Others try to form a path of escape. This is where alcohol and drugs can come in. The drowning out of pain or circumstances is a way to avoid facing reality. When a person refuses to face reality, "they just may not have to deal with it," or so they think. With alcohol and drugs the original problem can take on a new dimension, when abuse is added in the equation that is written for disaster. Still, the problem remains, depression looms and nothing is solved. Many people are victims of this reality. They wonder why they are not happy and are plagued with depression.

I believe it simply goes back to our being one with our world and circumstances. Both of which are undeniable, even when we try. In order for anything to be resolved, we must stop the covering up process and go back to the root of the problem. We must deal with our failures in a positive, corrective way, if at all possible. When doing so, it may just bring you out of depression and a state of looming failure. There are some things in life that we have no control over. There are some things in life that we cannot correct. When this happens, the best we can do, is walk in acceptance and forgive ourselves, if need be. To practice forgiveness is to show forth God's righteousness. The forgiving of oneself can be one of the hardest things to do. But, it is necessary if you are to move on and begin in the harmony and fullness of life; that God wants for you to have. We must stop muzzling the cries of our conscience. We must listen to the voice that tells us what you should be doing and do it. It is far better than a life that is stolen by unsuccessful attempts of covering up failures. Psalm 34: 17-18 "The righteous cry out and the Lord hears, and delivers them out of all of their troubles. The Lord is near to all those who have a broken heart, and saves such as have a contrite spirit."

GUARDING THE BODY FROM BLIGHT OF THE CHURCH

The story of blight is certainly not an unfamiliar one to God. The fact is that from times of old, God's people have had a tendency toward it. The book of Haggi has one of the most famous Passages in the Bible. "Is it then the right time for you to live in luxurious homes, when the temple lies in ruins?" says the Lord. (Haggai 1:3-4) While the blessings of America are abundant, many Christians have become preoccupied with the things in this life. They have put the work of the Lord on hold. My pastor recently shared with us that only one church out of 100, is actively reaching out trying, to win lost people to the Lord. How can this be, if blight and blind sightedness has not hit the church? The Mission of the church has been established by Christ Himself. It lies in the Great Commission. Go and tell . . . . baptizing others in the faith. (Matthew 28: 18-20) I wonder if Christians today some how have failed to understand that there is No exempt clause; on the obedience that is required of us to answer the command. The mission has been handed to us from God's own heart. We say that we love Jesus; yet we will walk by millions of people in our lifetime and hardly ever utter a word about Him, to any of them. In America and across the seas, people are dying everyday without Jesus. Yet we can be found tending to our own affairs in the preoccupation of our day! We act as if our world . . . is the only thing that truly matters.

I had the privilege of having lunch with a young missionary friend of mine. As we chatted, the subject of the church came up. She astounded me with her loving indictment of the church. "Why have church, if all we are going to do is have church and go home?" The true church is not just a building, for they are seeking the lost and helping the hurting and poor. Yet today some churches have lost their vision and turned inward. A church that does not come out of its' walls for Christ sake, can not be pleasing unto Him. Perhaps your church does not literally lay in ruins; as the temple did in the book of Haggi, but it is on the brink of spiritual ruin and devastation. Are their fights and power struggles? Have you lost your way;

without a clear vision from God? Are your hands tied by a controlling few? Does God have a voice and a receptive audience, where you are? Today, God can be found working through His people. A successful church must be tuned to God in prayer and seeking out His will for their lives. When God reveals His will, obedience must follow. Every church must follow Christ example. He was literally on foot for the Gospel. He sought out the needs of the people as He went by. Then, He attended to them. Scripture reveals a Righteous God; who ask His people to help the helpless and save the lost and dying. (Isa. 1:17) A church that is consumed with apathy and indifference faces the danger revealed in the book of Revelation. To be lukewarm, is to be spit out from the Master's mouth. (Rev. 3:14-21) True spiritual progress can only come when all hearts are tuned to the Master's plan. Then you will find your spiritual destiny given in your midst, from His heart to your hands and feet!

FALSE LEADERS IN THE MODERN CHURCH OF JESUS CHRIST

From the early beginning of the New Testament Church, problems and false leaders can be found. Some of the writings in the New Testament were to the church concerning false doctrines that were trying to be passed on to the followers of Christ. It has been an on going problem since the creation. Peter in particular was never shy about addressing the false teachings and setting the record straight. (2Pet. 2: 1-10) His head-on approach is an admirable way to clear the church of unwanted problems. False teachers will probably always try to infiltrate and mislead God's people, if it is possible. I know at my church our staff is on guard against such people. I can remember the story of my Pastor getting upset when someone came in asking to address our people. Another one of our Pastors came in to calm down the situation. If it can happen in Knoxville, Tennessee; it can happen anywhere. As I write this I have on my heart the Catholic Church, who has suffered over the misconduct of some priests. Scripture reveals a Righteous God Who promises to shine His Light in the darkness and expose it. That is in essence, what happened to some Catholic priests. It is never easy for Christians to see the dark side of life prevail. Many good Catholics have been stunned and they stand with their hearts laid open and bleeding. The question arises, "What do you do, when your church and the leaders participate in evil?" How can one continue to believe and find comfort? The universal belief is that the church is a safe harbor from the world. When the harbor is violated and your beliefs lay mutilated, where can you go? My heart goes out to the many Catholics around the world. God is aware of your pain. Since the beginning of creation, evil has co-existed with good. God's call has always been to come out from the world's desires to Him. God makes it clear in the book of Revelation that tolerating evil in the midst of the church is not pleasing unto Him. The Catholic Church has long been recognized, as the largest and most powerful church in the history of Christianity. This makes these events more disturbing.

One day, I had lunch with a young woman who stated that she was a Roman Catholic. She professed to have denounced her faith. After talking with her a while, I had to wonder if she was really saved at all. In view of the problems in her church, I understood her reaction. My concern for her was a much broader spiritual issue. In America we are given the freedom to make many choices. We may pick up and leave any situation at will. There is no doubt that evil can reshape the course of our lives. Fleeing from evil, to avoid bearing it's resemblance is appropriate at times. God's call has always been to Him and away from evil. As I reviewed my friend's situation, a word of caution surfaced in my being. This same word, I will give to all suffering Catholic Saints; "It is ok to reject a religion, but you better not reject a Savior." The real question of the hour is, "Who is the identity, that do you bear?" Is it the Catholic Church or Christ? We must remember there is a vast difference in the two. The church is made up of the body of Christ, the believers. Christ the Savior is Almighty God. The earthly church being a mix of man and God is flawed, at best. The Savior being God is perfect. One of the pursuits of Satan, has always been the church and its' people. Scripture reveals a creature who's purpose is to steal, kill and destroy. (John 10:10) Some of the obstacles we encounter in life can be attributed to Satan. His agenda for the main stream church among others is to destroy it. Renouncing the Catholic Church would be pleasing unto Satan. It is a much harder road to stay the course, in the middle of the trouble and turmoil. Discouragement is normal, when troubles plague our lives. Although in Scripture discouragement is attributed to Satan. The mark of all true Christian religions is to bear the likeness of the Savior. Trouble like this, should cause us to draw closer to the Savior, for His provisions. Our reaction must not be to spurn the creation of His Spirit, the church. We are called to be true and build up in Truth, the body of Christ. At times like this, we should dig in our heels and plant over traces of evil with His Goodness. Every denomination has had bouts with evil. False teachers and leaders have always had the agenda of the tearing down of the church. But good prevails when evil is exposed and the truly good and sanctified remain. It is by this process of God, that He purges out evil and sows eternal seeds of His Righteousness on earth. In Psalms 36: 5-12, God calls out to our souls to come to an unfailing God and feed in His abundance and love. Our eternal quest is to keep our eyes on Jesus, stay faithful to Him and allow His strength to supply all our needs, for all of the crisis times in our lives.

BE AN ACTIVE PART OF GOD'S BODY . . . USE YOUR GIFTS TO SERVE

One of the greatest things about America is our right to choose. So much of who we are today is a result of man's choices and of course, the Favor of God. Our right to be free comes from our forefathers drafting the constitution. Our abundance of light came from Einstein's choice to invent the light bulb. What would our world be like, if man had simply chosen not to act? All the productivity of the ages would simply not exist. Our modern conveniences would not surround us, and we more likely than not, would be in a state of hardship. Yet in the church of God, there are untold numbers of children that for one reason or another have chosen to hide their gifts and talents. They chose to store them away like some rare commodity. Can you imagine, Garth Brooks, never singing? What if the "Wizard of Oz" movie had just been a good idea? Just think for a moment, of all the things that we would have missed out on!

The Scripture makes it clear that the church is God's body. (1Cor. 12: 27-31) We all are given talents and gifts. The idea is that without all of us using our gifts, the function of the body is incomplete. I like the saying of our Pastor, when a person joins, "We have something to offer a family and they have something to offer us that we are in need of." Even if you are not aware of it, if you are a Christian you have been gifted by the Lord and His Spirit for the work of God on earth and in the church. It is God's desire that you would find your gift thus fulfilling your place in the mission and body of the church. Without understanding of this nature, one will feel incomplete and perhaps like they do not fit in. When you know your calling, you can then in confidence, do the work.

However, the freedom to act comes with responsibility. We must be careful to make choices that honor God. The fear of God, in our choices, illustrates true wisdom. When we take responsibility for our actions, we will weigh out the impact of our actions on others. I have observed in my years in the church many faithful followers of Christ. I have also found others who seem to lack in love for people, in their service. Even some who have been unkind or harsh. We must remember that our greatest calling is to love God and people. Ministry that is done without the ingredient of love falls short of pleasing God. (1Cor. 13) A person, who hinders God's work by having no love for people, should realize that without love, they have no real ministry at all. True ministry flows from the heart of God and is drenched in His love and attends the needs of others, in the name of Christ.

My challenge to the body of Christ is to get busy in His Name. Walk in love and in His Power, to reach out to others, in this world. Find your gift and talents and use them, for they will fulfill your hearts desire. Joy will be the result of the giving away, of yourself. Don't be found robbing the church of your gifts and talents; by not taking the opportunities that God already has prepared, for those who want their lives to be found leaving behind the footprints of the pathway to God.

STANDING TRUE TO YOURSELF
AND YOUR GOD

As I write this chapter tonight, I have a totally different kind of peer pressure to talk to you about. It is the pressure that families and close friends have on us. Perhaps, Dad is a third generation policeman so; you find pressure to be the next one in line. Or, maybe your sister is multi-talented and excels in everything. And, when you see yourself, you can't see any gifts that stand out. I call it the cookie cutter life style. If you feel like you are lost and can't find your way, that is not such a bad thing after all! The truth is that all of us are created by God, for HIS PURPOSES. Our quest is to find out, what that involves in our life. We all are as different, as our fingerprints are unique. That is why a cookie cutter mold does not work for all families. In fact, this kind of pressure can be very destructive. The sense of not measuring up can set in on a young person's heart and mind; or even worse, the sense of failure. Please, parents allow your children all the love and freedom to choose, that you can. Praise and recognition is an immeasurable goodness that fosters success in children. God must figure into your equation for what the future holds. It is of utmost importance, to realize that God has a plan for each of our lives. Your path may be completely different from anything around you. Just because someone did things this way or that, doesn't mean that you have to do the same. It is possible that the plan for your life can only be revealed by Jesus. Prayer and seeking God's Will and Word will assist you, in finding your way. The footsteps of Jesus are what you are to follow, not necessarily anyone else's! I am in no way saying, that you shouldn't listen to others around you. But, the best path is one paved in prayer and walking in the assurance of peace in your heart. If your journey is not one of peace of heart, it is possible that you are walking in the wrong direction. The lack of peace in any situation, can be the Spirit's way of telling you, "Wrong way . . . GO back!" As a general rule, I try to never violate the peace that is in my heart. God promises His children peace, for those who hearts and minds are trusting in Him. (Isa. 26:3) (Ps 85:8) I do believe that our God can and does open and close doors for His children. One secret to finding His purposes where you are is to walk in faith and serve Him where He sends you. When Christ was on earth, His ministry was on the move. He used the opportunities as they presented themselves. Like Christ, some chances to minister or witness may only come once, in our lifetime. Cowering to the possibility of fear or failure may result in the loss of God's using you, in someone's life. (1Pet. 3:15)

Sometimes, God uses your words to play over and over in a person's mind. You can never underestimate the power of words. Words that are ordained of God, can very easily, bring fruit in another's life. Or, they could direct a person in another whole different direction. You might find that you have a confirmation that someone is waiting on. Only God really knows all the ways He wants to use you, while you are there. This is another reason why you can not take a cookie cutter approach to life. You are not everyone else, you belong to God. God's Word makes it clear that He ordains and directs our path. Walking with God and being a vessel that He can use for His glory, may be one of the meanings of living the abundant life. I have heard it said that if someone ask you about God or spiritual things, God is working in their life. This means, you are on course and experiencing God's perfect timing. You are the chosen vessel for the opportunity. But, also just as important are the times, when people open up to you about their hurts or problems. This is your chance to point them in the direction of God. (Col. 3: 15) One thing that is indisputable is your testimony of what God has done for you! Christ is and holds the answers to all of life. One has to wonder, how many times, we all have missed the opportunity of a life time; to do a little planting of God's seeds or healing words, in the soul's of hurting or searching people!

The challenge that is set before us is to stay alert! Ask God to open our ears and eyes, to what He is saying through others around us. Yes, we have the time! No excuses! To fail to minister, to the hurting people around us, could very well mean that we missed our purpose for that God given day! Finding the right pathway cut uniquely just for you by God, will result in realizing your deepest levels of contentment and purpose.

SPEAK THE NAME OF JESUS; PLANT THE SEEDS

Can you imagine the impact on the world if the disciples had never written or spoken a word? What if the transformed Apostle Paul never uttered a word about Jesus? Where would the world/we be today? Is it possible that many of the people of God will go through their lives, hardly uttering a word to anyone about God? They have never really realized, their God given mission field. Spiritual blindness can result in the loss of thousands of opportunities, over the period of a lifetime. Our conversations can be the planting fields, for the seeds of God. We should always remember that only God can water and give the increase. (1Cor. 3:7) The results of which, we may never see. But, God knows of our part and the outcome. I can't help but wonder, what would happen if millions of believers began to just speak the Name of Jesus all over the world?

It is high time to speak the Name of Jesus when:
Lives are broken or death comes,
Marriages are failing or the injured are showing their pain,
Finances are failing or tragedy of any kind visits a family or friend,
Miracles occur; Praise the Name of Jesus,
Good jobs are given; Praise the Name of Jesus,
When a birth takes place; Praise the Name of Jesus,

The Bible tells us that all good gifts are from the Father of Heavenly Lights. (Js 1:17) Jesus is never defeated, wherever we find ourselves. He is simply never caught off guard, by our circumstances. Please know that our All Knowing God has a plan where ever you find yourself. Acknowledge Him in prayer and faith. Then, walk on. He will take care of you! Today, unlike any time in the world, people are looking for hope. The world's hope for a good life lies in Jesus. It is up to us to point the way. One of the greatest sins a Christian can be guilty of is, "God Silence!" How can others know, if they have not heard, because we refuse to share. Many people are afraid of losing friends, if they talk about Jesus. I am afraid of losing friends eternally, if I don't talk! Life style evangelism is not enough, if it is not backed up with loving words and actions that point to its Source. God has given me a heart of concern for others need of salvation. I can't seem to accept the alternative of Hell, for those who reject Jesus. (Matt. 13:37-43) One of my first concerns for a stranger or friend is if they are going to heaven with me. I don't mind telling someone, that I want to take them with me to heaven. God has blest me with the opportunity to lead others to Christ. I hope that through them, thousands of others will come to know Him. God promises us a new heart and His mind, after our salvation. (Ezek. 36:26, 1Cor. 2:16) We must take a hold of all that is promised to us by faith. If, we will prayerfully start the day asking for His eyes, ears, heart and mind, then we will be closer to closing the gap of missed opportunities. So, speak the Name of Jesus as God intended, to those He has given around you. Pray for the planted seed because only God can yield the harvest. (John 4:34-37) (John 15:16)

TO ALL THE HURTING CHILDREN . . . .
GOD IS CALLING YOU!

Well, it is Christmas, a time of joy and celebration! As I sit here, in front of my Christmas tree, all the children of the world are on my heart. So many children can lose their way. It can happen so easily. If you are hurting tonight, there is ONE Who cares for You! His name is Jesus. Living life apart from Jesus can be dark and lonely. To choose a life without Him is to have one that is empty of real joy and meaning. Sometimes in life, Jesus is all we have. Jesus tells us in His Word, that His grace is sufficient for all our needs. (2 Cor. 12:9) If you are in need of healing or hope, it can begin with a simple prayer to Him. Time and time again, I have heard my friends say, "We don't know what people do, without Him/ Jesus." He has helped us through our most difficult times by being our Best Friend.

If you feel alone and that no one cares for you, you need to know that He cares for You! If your world has turned up side down, He cares for you! If everyone in your life has turned against you, He cares for you! When people mistreat you and put you down, He cares for you! The lyrics, "The world was dark and lonely, till He appeared and the soul felt its' worth," comes to mind. Now . . . because He came we can know Him in a personal way. I treasure the saying, "This is how much I love you . . . and He stretched out His arms and died" . . . . just for You! Jesus died to give victory to all of those who will come to Him. Jesus is for you, when others fail you because they are human. Jesus waits for you to come to Him with your needs. So much so, that He sits at the right hand of God the Father and intercedes for us. The book of Hebrews calls Him our Great High Priest. (Heb. 4:15) Jesus, left the glories of heaven and appeared to us. He is the Greatest Gift that has ever been given to mankind! He came to earth, because His love for us motivated Him to appear among us. He wants to show us the way of "True Life" . . . . in Him. He wants to meet our deepest needs. He is the Great "I AM" . . . (Gen. 26:24) the All Powerful Victorious One. His life on earth is the greatest evidence, of His caring for us. In His death on the Cross for our sins, He has proven to be the Greatest Love Of All Times! (Ps.17:7)

Today, Jesus life, death and resurrection, still calls out to everyone to come to Him. The pardon is free . . . . for He has already attended to the debt, that we owe. It is our job to accept what He has done for us. Calvary, the place of our Lord's death, made it possible for all who will, to be made friends with God eternally. It is a friendship unlike any other . . . as it never ends and is eternal in nature. The fountain of blood that flows from His veins from Calvary never ends. It has the power to wash and make you new. You can not lose what Jesus has done on Calvary. The Word says it this way . . . "No one can be snatched, from His hands." (John 10:28-29) Jesus is the Sweet Savior of Fellowship, who wants to make an eternal residence in your heart. Jesus is the Man who is fully God and man, Who knows you completely. Yet, in spite of all your failings, He loves you always! If you will allow Him to come into your heart and life, He will gladly partner with you, in all areas of your life. I like to say, "He will be in everything that you will allow Him to be in!" He will stand closer to you than a brother. His love is more powerful than a mother. He is stronger than any dad on earth. He is more loyal than any person or favorite animal on earth. When you allow Him into your heart, as your Savior, He is always present with you and full of love for you! Whatever the world throws in your way . . . read His Word and you can discern the lies and know the Truth. His presence in your life will transform your being, as you allow His Spirit to partner with you in life. What ever the need, where ever you find yourself . . . . just a little prayer to Jesus can renew your hope and change your perspective on everything. Jesus, our Best Friend, brightens our lives, renews our hope and strengthens us. He will lighten our load and renew our peace. Such gifts as these and more are His to give to His children. Jesus is a Mighty Conqueror, full of Power and Light. Submission to such a power in prayer makes our yoke with Him light and easy. (Matt. 11:30) The Word testifies to us that we are loved. As our Father, He wants us to follow, hope and trust Him. (Ps. 37:3) (John 14: 1) Though the voice of the world may try to crush or destroy us, we will not receive their truth. To do so, would be to exchange the Real Truth for a lie. He is the Good Shepherd that wants to always tend to our every need. We are to receive His words of love and affirmation. As His children, we are to throw off the voices of hatred and those who disdain or want to trample us. Instead, we are to listen to the Great Shepherd Who abides with us, with a heart filled with love for us. In the safety of such love, His children/you will thrive. Praise be to God, Who's love compelled Him to appear to us, that we might know Him and the richest of His love.

If you are hurting tonight, turn to Jesus. It is always His hope that you will come to Him. We can not heal ourselves. Without our Master's touch our lives are broken. When we surrender our lives to Him, we begin to inherit all the riches that we have already been given in Christ. Which will you choose? The choice is yours to make. To choose wisely and come to the Savior is to enter your destiny of love, hope and self worth. Jesus had His eye on you, when He came to dwell among us. Will you come to Him now, please! I am sure that He is calling you!

Remember this: You are . . . .

NEVER ALONE	HE ABIDES WITH YOU
NEVER DOWN TRODDEN	HE WILL LIFT YOU UP
NEVER ABANDONED	HE PROMISES TO NEVER LEAVE YOU
NEVER BEYOND HIS REACH	HIS LIFE AND DEATH WAS FOR ALL
NEVER WITHOUT HOPE	AN ALL POWERFUL SAVIOR WHO CARES
NEVER WITHOUT POWER	A PERSONAL INDWELLING SPIRIT/POWER
NEVER WITHOUT WISDOM	HIS WORD IN US . . . HIS WILL, BE DONE
NEVER WITHOUT BLESSING	HIS PROMISE TO BLESS AND RECEIVE US
NEVER WITHOUT A FUTURE	HIS PROMISE OF BLESSINGS & A FUTURE

Deut. 31:6, Matt. 12:20, Deut. 4:31, Ps. 36:5-10, Mic. 7:7, 1Sam. 10:6-7, James 1:5, Deut. 28:1-14, Jer. 29:11-13.

Oh, what a God can be found, when we turn our heart and minds to Him in repentance, faith and obedience. He promises, "Seek and you will find, knock and the door will be opened." His heart for us is to give us hope, a future and His blessings in everything.

CAPTURED IN ANXIETY OR STANDING IN FAITH?

Are you familiar with sleepless nights? Those times when all you can do is toss and turn. If you are like me, you have prayed yourself out, yet your mind still will not yield to sleep. For me, my schedule and all the things I know must get done tomorrow, will keep me awake. Or maybe, it is the hardship and burdens of others that lays on your heart and restless mind. Millions of people all across our land wrestle with stress, anxiety and even depression. The reasons are as complex as each situation that wants to capture and overwhelm us. I want to share with you my story of panic, that hit a few years ago. In 1990, I started working for my husband doing his billing. I needed something part time to do and the billing needed someone to attend to it. I had worked on computers for years, and offered to put all of the accounts on it for them. The company bought some accounting software. The cost was around $500.00. Things were going well, a few months into the adventure. One day, I tried to copy the master, for a back up and destroyed it instead! Talk about panic, all I could think about was the price tag! I knew that I was dead! Right in the middle of a total panic, the Lord spoke to me. He said softly, "Do you trust Me?" Over and over He repeated this question to my panicked heart. I finally answered Him, "Yes Lord." Then He added, "Look back over your life, have I ever let you down?" The answer was, "NO!" He had convinced me in these two short phrases to trust Him! I had to find the right time and tell Joel. I knew that I also, had to call the company that sold us the software too. Joel took the news well. It seemed he just wanted to help me find the solution. After praying, I finally worked up faith and courage to call the California software company. The Lord was with me and it went well. The person on the phone explained to me that they had just deleted the software. However, they would send me one more master . . . . FREE! After that, "I was on my own!" God provided, just as He promised. I was given favor and my need was taken care of. Think just for another minute about this story. God had also arranged just the right person, to answer the phone 3,000 miles away. One who would care and help me resolve the problem, of my own making! There was at least a 50% chance that someone else could have answered and just stated the facts. The software was deleted. But no . . . favor was given and all went really well for me! Think about the love of a God, who moments before was silently abiding. Then panic struck, and He softly addressed His child and called her to trust. That is the heart of my Father!

I learned that day about His concern and love. I found Him to care and want to show provision, in a time of crisis. I also learned the skill of looking backwards, to an Unfailing God of Love! That day, I learned about panic. I also, found a God who took it up for me, immediately. This day, I would never forget! The lesson is of an Abiding God, who meets His children, where they are. He delivers them to safety and provision. That day, I learned to look back over my shoulder, not panic. I have a totally Reliable God, Who is my Refuge and Strong Tower. He wants me to simply, trust Him. And, if I am tempted to panic, I will just look back over my shoulder to see again, His unfailing love once more!

Our God is an All Powerful God. He delights in helping His children. You are dearly loved by Him. Even, when you are not aware of it, He is abiding with you. He calls us unto Himself, to gain knowledge of Him. He wants to give and has promised favor on your life. He rewards consistent faith, earnest prayer and reliance on Him. If you find yourself in a jam, I challenge you to take it to the Lord. You will find your power and solutions there.

The emotions of fear and anxiety are not components of faith. They are in fact, exact opposites of it. They are apart of the human condition. They are emotions, all of us have experienced in the course of life. It is in those uncomfortable situations and uncharted territories that can bring on such emotions. We must be careful, not to let these emotions master us. They are not of faith. God promises to cast out fear, with perfect love. He wants to give a sound mind. "For God has NOT given us a spirit of fear, but of Power and of Love and of a Sound Mind." (2Tim. 1:7) Finding and standing on His promises in faith helps to deliver us, in times that wear us down and tests us. Remember that God is faithful to His Word. A child that holds His Word in their hands and believes it in their heart, is on the path, where God shows up!

I can remember another night that rest was not in sight. I checked the clock and it was 4:00 a.m. I laid in bed and decided, "Surely God has something, He wants to say to me." I got up and went to the recliner with my Bible in hand. I opened it and soon found myself in the book of Job. I was stunned at what I read there! I could not lay it down. The discourse blew my mind. God talked to Job about things that have never entered my mind! He talked to him as the Creator to the created. If you have a problem with anxiety and fear, I challenge you to read Job/ Chapters 38-41. After reading God's response to Job, I was calmed in my spirit, once again. My conclusion was, "We the created are in good hands!" Hands that are able to completely take care of us, if we will only trust and believe. God is able to deliver you from all of your cares, if you will ask, trust and believe to receive!

A WORD TO THE CRUSHED IN SPIRIT;
SET YOUR HEART ON JESUS.

Where does life find you today? Are you in a good place or sitting there in hurt that is beyond belief? Does if feel like everyone has let you down? Are you sad because the pain is great and you feel all alone? Maybe even those closest to you have been a source of great disappointment. If you find yourself there, then there is good news for you! First of all you can fix the fact that you feel all alone! A child of God is never alone and he or she is a child of promise! God assures of His presence daily in His Word. He desires to walk with you every step of the way. He will supply our every need with His strength. His heart is to keep us close to Him and bless us. He has given us a source of encouragement for our daily lives. A written source of Truth, hope, light, comfort and joy that is ours for the taking. We can have as many helpings as we want or need. The Bible is designed to fill us with many good blessings for living. Its' power enriches and restores our soul. It reveals to us a wonderful and worthy God. One who will never give up on us and can be found always calling us unto Himself. In Him alone can one find eternal life, happiness, peace, healing and strength. Gifts such as these belong only unto Him. He longs to give freely to those who love Him.

Resounding help, justice, righteousness, truth and love are the foundations of His Being. Triumph, victory, blessing and promises are His endowments. Freely He gives and freely He flows. His heart is one that will never disappoint us. He is able to give to us far above what we could ever think to ask of Him! As we get serious about Him, He will get serious with us. He died to make us heirs to all that He owns. In His time, He will deliver us safely to our heavenly home with Him. He personally will attend the way, when He calls us there. Our God is the only One that is truly worthy of our lives and will crown us with eternal life. Yes, He has allowed for our lives to be a journey that He will supply our every need. If you will but follow Him, He will personally lead the way. He can change the whole course of your life and give to you a glorious outcome. If you are tired and weary, He is the one that can and will renew your strength.

Jesus has been my Trustworthy Friend, for as long as I can remember. I know in my heart that I will never have to give Him up! Just as He has promised, I will see Him, one day face to face. He is the God of Wonder and Glory. The One who loved me more than He loved His life on earth; as He gave up His life just for you and I.

Jesus wants to help you now, where ever you find yourself. He is able to bring you where you need to be. In Him alone, is found new and never ending life. He is the missing ingredient of an abundant life. He is the Stability and Hope that all of creation needs. Our Source Book exclaims that in Him alone is found glory and eternal life. A glory and power that begins when He is allowed to take up residence in our heart. Will you please allow Him to come in? His desire is to fill your heart and enrich your life with true joy and contentment. Such gifts of your soul can only be found in Him. He, the Author of all of creation says that we reap what we sow. This is an eternal principle that yields or fails according to the chosen path of our own making. Much awaits you, if you will call on His name. One thing He can promise is that your life will never be the same. Join us and become a Child of Promise and an Heir from a Heavenly King. He has His arms outstretched to you and full of gifts and benefits. He has given His all to everyone who will listen and come. Remember that the outcome is of your own making, for the choice is yours to make. Oh, children may each of you and your families be found completely standing in Him, on the day and hour of His certain second coming! (Isa. 42:3) A bruised reed He will not break, and a smoldering wick He will not snuff out. Only our Living God can say one simple sentence and it be words that you feel like shouting to everyone, from the rooftops!

BAGGAGE AND ESSENTIAL
FORGIVENESS

"Baggage" now there is a word that conjures up all kinds of images. From struggles at an airport to the struggles of the soul. One thing that you can be sure of is that God does not want baggage, for anyone of us. However, in the process of living every day life and it's struggles, baggage can appear. If we are not careful, we can carry around our load until we are too weary to continue. Often unrecognized baggage can become a controlling force in our lives; a force that if left unchecked can ruin our relationships. Baggage can load us up in heavy weights and slow or stop us right in our tracks. The question arises, "How does one break the cycle of baggage?" We must recognize that apart from Godly introspection, we may never be free. The Bible commands us to examine ourselves to see if we remain in faith. Such an internal audit can reveal our hidden motives, damages and it's sources. Prayer is one of the most powerful weapons that we have against baggage. It is also one of the best ways to free ourselves from unwanted entanglements. When we experience His light on our pain, struggles and hurts then . . . understanding is on it's way to us. When we understand where we are and how we got there, then we can begin to experience healing to our deepest needs. Jesus wants to heal and help us. The wise person will choose to put Him at the center of their work. He purposefully chose to be our Intercessor and Advocate to the Father. His power over us is our guarantee, that the process will work for us. Sometimes our process is found in taking baby steps daily. When we choose to conscientiously place our faith in God over the matters that concern us, this in itself is freeing. Who told us that our problems were created for us to solve? The Scripture leans more to the side that struggles are for the building of hope, faith and character in us. I have always like the idea of life lessons. Lessons that when we learn them, we will never have to repeat them. I like the idea of learning the lessons that others have experienced too.

Forgiveness is an essential process in our healing. Whether it be towards ourselves or others, it is essential in healing our hurts. Baggage will remain apart from completing the process of forgiveness. The journey may be one of the most painful ever, but the rewards are worth the cost. I believe that the journey of forgiveness is one of the wisest choices a person can make. Wholeness, tranquility and peace are unveiled in it's practice. These are so worth the time and effort. After all we are talking about the quality of our and our loved ones lives.

Don't let baggage rob you of your life in the present. Get on your hands and knees before God. Give Him all of your struggles. Give Him your broken heart. Surrender to Him in faith all of your problems and concerns. He wants to hear all of them. Pray about everything, having confidence that He cares for you. Keep repeating the process until you have emptied yourself out before Him. Then come up in faith, leaving it all at His feet. You have given Him your problems and He is able to handle them for you. Tell God that you will watch for Him. Refuse to take them back, when they try to plague your heart and mind. Affirm that all your heart concerns and struggles have been laid at the Master's feet. Praise Him for what He will do. So many times we relinquish to God the matters of our heart, only to pick them up again. We must remember that we serve an All Powerful God, who is able to help us even when we can not help ourselves. "The battle is mine," says the Lord. (Deu. 3:22) "I will fight for you." (2Chron. 20:15) What we need to never forget is that He is able and willing to help us, if we will allow Him too. We must keep our position in faith trusting in His love and power over our lives. Those who stand in faith and surrender in obedience will see the hand of God move.

As I am writing this, my heart feels for the person that has become overwhelmed with life's problems. One thing that is for certain, things are going to change. If you are wondering if life is really worth living, I would say to you a resounding, "YES!" Don't give up just because you can't see the Master's plan for your life. You see life has a way of preparing us for our future, if we will only co-operate and stay in faith. Some avenues we would never have arrived on, if not for the twists and turns of our life. And even if you did, you wouldn't be the person that you are now, for having lived thru it all. Only God sees the Master weaving of our soul. We just become a quality person who is like God and cares for others. Change is never easy. Especially if the direction is one that you don't want to go in. There was a time in my life that things fell apart for me. I was happy and doing good things for God. Then I found myself uprooted completely and cut off. It was painful, but I knew that God was still in charge over me. I knew in my heart that I had to accept this change. As His child, I trusted that in all reality, God had been the one to move me, because He has authority over me. My life belongs to Him. I knew that one day I would be glad for the change that was coming my way. He helped me to continue to trust Him in all of these things. I can honestly say that if God had not moved me, I would never be writing this book! I simply would not have found or made the time. I believe that our God interrupted me for a much greater purpose that even at that time, I could have ever seen! Today, I have no regrets! When I really look at it, I was not totally happy like I thought. But today, I can say I am so glad to be able to write to you all and proclaim the God that I know and love! One thing we must always remember is that our God is never caught off guard, in relation to our lives. He is never without a plan or purpose in mind for us. Only God can take the bad and weave beauty into our hearts and minds. Our job is to stay the course in faith and allow Him to prepare us for His plan for our future.

Even if you don't know what to do next, don't take the bait and give up on life. Such promptings are never from God. God's words assures us that He is for us and He wants to bless us in ways we may have never experienced. If your plan folds before your eyes, keep the faith. God has a way and a more perfect plan for you. Don't destroy your life. God wants to bring you close and reveal Himself to you! His hands are never empty of the good things that He has for you. If you are at the end of your rope and simply do not know what to do with your life, just give it to the Lord Jesus. He WILL bring you thru to see His Goodness and plan for your life. There are times when we have "to be still and know that He is God" and our Refuge. Stand true to Him and wait for His perfect plan. You can be sure that He knows what you are going thru and that He loves you! He is never defeated by your circumstances. A faithful contrite heart, He will not overlook. One thing that I know is that life is about God bringing you where He wants you to be. One day you will be in the center of His will and find yourself thanking Him for His Master Plan. You belong to Him. If you don't know God, then please give Him a try, He died for you! He is worthy of you! He loves you more than any love you have ever known on earth. He promised that He will be found by you, when you search for Him! His plan is the best that life has to offer. Wait on Him and you will see and be glad. His love and mercy never fails!

EXPOSING THE TRAP OF; DESTROYING GOD'S TEMPLE.

America has been blest with our share of young and beautiful girls. I am writing to you as an older women, hoping to encourage your faith. Many of you are doing well. Hopefully you are vibrant and healthy. There are many mixed messages trying to get your attention. Strong messages of sex and beauty are paraded in front of you, at every angle. With these voices comes the pressure to conform to the standards of the day. I am hoping that you will not take the bait and be misled. Many young women have listen and found themselves captured in the endless consequences of bulimia and anorexia. If you are in this battle alone, I am reminding you that there is a better way to live. You don't have to walk this life alone. God watches and waits for you! If you are a Christian, I want you to realize that your body is the temple of the Holy Spirit. I Corinthians 3:16-17, says that we are not to destroy God's temple.

In our society, with the tremendous pressure, young women are judged by their looks and fitness. Some women have believed, at all cost, "thin is where it is at." As a wise Pastor once said, "they are listening to the wrong voices." The Bible plainly states that all of us, are created by God in His image. God created us, for Himself. It was by His design, that we would come to know, love and have intimate fellowship with Him. Being His creation, all of us are very special to Him! If your circumstances are such that you feel, "No one cares" . . . this news is for you! In the Garden of Eden, when Adam and Eve had just sinned and caused all of creation to fall . . . God came near! Today all of us are living out the consequences of their actions, yet our God who is Faithful, can be found calling and seeking them unto Himself! What a glorious and powerful picture of eternal Truth and love can be found here! The LORD OF HEAVEN AND EARTH, can be found today, still calling and seeking out those who will listen! In full view of all our faults, God cares and seeks to love us. The concept of a Supernatural God, who loves us and wants a personal relationship with us, in spite of all that we are, is a thrilling prospect of truth for all of us.

Allowing God in and making time to know His heart and the depths of His love, will result in a life that is happier and more at peace.

When I was in Junior High, a boy let me know that he was attracted to me. He was a popular person. His attraction to me caught me off guard. It was the first time that I had ever heard the saying, "Beauty is in the eye of the beholder." Looking back, I can see the truth of that statement. True beauty that God looks for resides in the heart and mind of one that carries out their life, in the walk of love. Man looks on the outward appearance, but God looks at the heart. (1Sam 16:7) True beauty, that will never fade is the beauty of the inner spirit of a women, that has been touched by God. If a women allows herself to love God and others with all of her heart and soul, she will have a radiant beauty from within. This beauty will not fade away, as with age. It is the beauty of Christ and His Likeness that radiates through her. This is the beauty that is eternal, true and worth seeking.

I know that God does want us to take care of our bodies and be fit, simply because excessive weight, can trip disease. But, to embrace the idea that one is to be thin at all cost is wrong. I would much rather be healthy looking than, sick and too thin. The real truth is that men like curves. God wants His people to be happy and healthy. Therefore, tearing down your body to be thin is wrong. Nutrition is a subject that we could all learn more about. The reason that we eat is to provide our bodies with health and energy. A diet that is healthy and feeds our body with nutrition should be our goal. To accept bulimia and anorexia as a way of life, is to trade away ones' true health and believe a distorted view of beauty. I want to ask all young women to look at eating in a different way. It is the providing of nutrition for your body to grow strong healthy and beautiful. Likewise, as you grow, you will be carrying a right relationship with food to care for your family's health. It would be great if dieticians would step forward in the churches and communities. We never get too old for education on eating healthier and building strong bodies. Tips for slimming down, would be greatly appreciated and help a lot of struggling people. A ministry of great value could easily be found in a country of rampant obesity and disease. Everyone can prosper with basic and new information to maintain a healthy body and lifestyle. Another area that I would like to see put out there is the knowledge of how to cook foods in a more heart healthy way and how to reduce fat in a recipe.

Girls in closing, remember that true beauty that stands the tests of time is from God. The Highest Power on earth and in heaven proclaims that YOU are special and loved! Our God, who took the time to fashion you after Himself, wants you to take care of yourself. This is honoring to God. If you find that you need help, ask for it. A woman who is healthy, vibrant, and well possesses an inner beauty that is the most beautiful women on earth! I challenge you to be well mentally/emotionally and seek out the best path for your body. Bring nourishment to your table and have beautiful vibrant spiritual health. When you do, you will be a real master piece of God. Then, you can help to shatter the myth that the tearing down and destroying of the body is real beauty. You can join in the fight to help set the captives free!

A FOUR FOLD CRISIS HITS HOME

As we look around it is not hard to find Americans who are having tough times, everywhere. It looks like Washington is broken. That is what they are saying on the news. I certainly agree with that assessment. Again, rebate checks are on the way. It is a nice gesture but really does little to solve the huge problems that are looming over our heads. It is clear that America needs help. But, at the same time some Leaders are missing the signs of the crisis. We need change desperately. I want to expand on each crisis individually. Here are the four folds of our crisis.

1) The War and Terrorism
2) The Energy/Gasoline crisis
3) The Drug crisis
4) The Health Care and Insurance crisis

The threat of terrorism and the war are taking a strong toll on our people. The cost of the war is worrisome. The uncertainty of the length of the war brings its on threats to our economy. Although, I am for delivering the world of terrorist; but at the same time, I am very uncomfortable about absorbing most of the cost. When you really look at it, the idea of years of war, it seems like it could break our economy. When so much is at stake under such a large issue, Americans stop or slow down on spending. Quick missions and moving out our troops would seem more like victory and progress. Perhaps, while keeping the next target in sight. To hear from the President of Iran, one could easily wonder, if we went into the wrong country. How will we pay for a one hundred year war? Who will fight it? What condition will our military and country be in? Will we survive it? These are the thoughts on the hearts and minds of many Americans. It seems, the war itself is a real threat to our well being!

The next crisis we face is an energy/gasoline crisis. In Tennessee under TVA, it takes hundreds of dollars a month, just to pay your light bill. This bill alone could take one whole pay check for some. Every time we turn around, rates are going up. Next gas is sky rocketing. A tank of gas is now a record $50.00. While gas and oil companies are reporting record profits. It is just another drain on the every day man. It seems like America, has another real threat on our homeland. How is it possible that record billions of dollars a quarter in profits are making Gas/Oil companies rich and individuals poor in the greatest country on earth? Why is it legal to take advantage of our people, in a society such as ours? And, no one addresses or corrects the problem. It is clear that we are being taken advantage of, on our own soil. It all connects back to a country that is too dependant on foreign oil. We desperately need to develop new energy sources. Perhaps, an alternative energy method would lower the cost of energy, since it would bring new market alternatives. To continue without progress in this area, in sight of the rising cost reflected in almost every area of our lives, is dangerous. It is like hanging a noose around our country's neck. We are failing to see that we could be chocked to economic failure at any time. This kind of power over us is dangerous. It simply must not be allowed to continue. With technology like it is and the great minds we have, surely alternative energy formulations can be produced. America has alot on the line with this particular problem. Energy source problems radiates into our pocketbooks that are already stressed and into almost every other economic area. It is time to wake up and fix the problems here, to provide the safety and security of all following generations. The car industry would have the most to gain with coming up with a solution. Americans may just be five times more interested in a super efficient car than they ever were before. So go for it, bring us the fuel crisis answer. One that would help with the air that we breathe and save us a bundle of cash! Your companies could potentially make economic history with the unveiling of the solution to us. No other industry has more that could be gained than you do. Lets not forget the truckers and their needs in this area either! We all drive and are in need of a better way both today and tomorrow!

The third unattended crisis is the widely existing drug crisis. The only area of concern expressed by our Press is for the seniors. This should not be! With the taxing burdens above . . . this problem further diminishes our financial well being. It would seem that the only people that are not suffering due to the high cost of drugs, are the wealthy. And, I am sure that even they would prefer not to have such high costs, on what for many is necessities.

Consider for a moment this scenario:
You go into the drug store and you find that one prescription is $100.00. You do not have drug coverage. Your health requires that you need six different prescriptions. Is anyone seeing the picture yet? This is on top of all the other expenditures above. How can anyone be comfortable about our future? This picture is a common one. Sometimes, you hear how people are having to choose between food and medicine. With the cost of needed medication drowning our income, it presents its' own leg of financial devastation. It is easy to see, that with unchecked economic balances such as these, the future is very uncertain now, for most Americans.

The fourth and last drain of our wealth is the heath care and insurance crisis. The insurance cost of operating a business is spiraling out of control. For some companies, this cost alone can be $50,000 to $200,000 a year or more. Is there any wonder that small businesses are closing their doors. These are otherwise healthy businesses that would have made it, if these cost could have been contained. The cost of personal healthcare, is also fast becoming unaffordable to many Americans. There are reported millions that are now not covered, with any insurance. If you look at these situations, how is it possible that we can afford to treat uninsured Americans, without breaking the healthcare industry? Our family has personally found a time when it was unaffordable to have personal health insurance. The cost many years ago went as high as $700.00 a month. How can we expect people to be able to afford all of these expenses and survive? No one person should be uninsured. Groups for all Americans should exist, if we have to cross state lines to do it, with national/international coverage. Perhaps it is time for national health care groups to be formed in all sectors, so that no one will be left uncovered. Such examples come to mind: National Healthcare for Truckers, National Health Care for Medical personnel, National Healthcare for Automobile workers. You get the picture? These skyrocketing problems, if left unattended could easily cripple our economic future.

Today more than ever, we need in touch leaders. Leaders equipped with powerful problem solving leadership. Men and women, who are not afraid to tackle hard tasks. Leaders of vision; who are not afraid to confront near impossible challenges. Step forward brilliant and tough, technology driven leaders. Are you one who will come out swinging and bring a new path of victory, against what ails us? Without leadership with these qualities, we have yet to see, the hardest of times that could so easily paralyze our country. It is time that all of us, including our leaders pay close attention to the reality of our times. Many promises for many years have been made about healthcare. No real solutions have been found. Even if children are covered, what quality of life do they have; when their parents are not and they are sick? We are not only leaving behind our children, but our whole society in general, when we fail to comprehend and solve all of these great financial burdens. What is Real Leadership . . . when it promises and fails to deliver . . . . time and time again, at the peril of a whole society? We desperately need leadership that has every American at the heart of their agenda. If as President Obama says . . . that to find our way, we must take on the lobbyist in Washington and their millions of dollars, to overcome our problems; then I say, such funding from large companies, is a conflict of interest for our leaders. We need to step back and realize that our government is of the people for the people and such large money flows for special interest that impedes our progress should be made illegal. Such a large conflict of interest simply should not be able to find a safe harbor, at the expense of all the American people.

I challenge all of us, including our leaders to pay close attention to the reality of our times. How can true leadership ignore the crises that threaten to take us hostage. Not one of these crisis must escape our attention. It is time to direct your heart beat to the path that will liberate our people. Americans, who pays your handsome salaries, is due her return and freedom from these crises. This is one of our most crucial hours. Failing to remedy our problems may prove near fatal to the American lifestyle, as we know it.

2 Chronicles 7: 13-15

"When I shut up the heavens so that there is no rain or command locust to devour the land or send a plague among My people, if My people who are called by My Name will humble themselves and pray and seek My face and turn from their wicked way, then will I hear from heaven and forgive their sin and will heal their land. Now my eyes will be open and my ears attentive to the prayers offered in this place."

A FORE-GLANCE OF THE APPEARANCE
OF A GODLESS SOCIETY

As I sit on my bed, I have one final question on my mind. It concerns our freedom of expression and our buildings. It grieves me when people plot to destroy our established traditions in America. Such as the taking out of "one nation under God" from our Pledge of Allegiance. Or, "in God we trust" off our money. What about the taking down of the Ten Commandments from the court room? Some have said the Nativity must go from the lawns of our buildings; or Happy Holidays not Merry Christmas! The question we must confront is WHY? What is the hidden agenda of such people that want to tamper with such sacred traditions? There are some things that should never be tampered with or changed. They reflect the heart and soul of our people, past and presently. The founding evidence of who we are in our inner spirit. The real historical reflection of the heart of our people, and our journey as a country. Why then removed such evidences of the true essence of our People?

What is the good that could come out of it? I wonder why our buildings and historical religious traditions are not protected under our freedom of expression or speech? Do we need to amend our Constitution, to end the fight once and for all? As I ponder the motives of such people, only one clear vision arises . . . . The appearance of a Godless Society; and the erasing of every evidence, of our faith off of our establishments. A testimony that to future generations, could yield confusion, about our true identity as a nation. It would be the appearance of a bland and cold society at a glance. When one looks around at our buildings they show not one evidence of our true religious heritage, of Christian love and faith. May Our God have mercy on us, when it is all taken away without even a fight!

Who among us can fix such atrocity and confusion? Rise up America and protect the freedoms that you were born to inherit, paid for by the blood of our soldiers. Before our true spiritual heritage and traditions that reflect the Truly Free People we are . . . simply Vanish!

WHICH AMERICA ... DO YOU WANT?

While this book has undoubtedly testified to the Lord Jesus Christ and His very real Presence. Scripture also provides us with a second reality. A second father can also be found listed in the pages of the Word. Unfortunately, his children bear his resemblance too. (Gal. 6:7-8) His traits are destruction, lies, hatred and deception. His name is Satan. The Bible makes it clear that true children bear their master's marks. (John 8:44, Luke 6:43-45)

Matthew 6:24, tells us that no one can love two masters. You will love one and hate the other. Although love can be found in America, darkness certainly co-exists. Hatred, violence, murder and death flood the streets in America. One who chooses the dark side of life will reap darkness and destruction. Unfortunately their world touches our world too. Innocent people become victims in their quest for the darkness. Adultery is rampant and glamorized. Drugs and alcohol are claiming lives in our homes and schools. Divorce runs wild in our homes. Emotional pain, and illness conflicts the best of our minds across every state. Devastation from needless pain is inflicted carelessly in the hearts of our youngest and most innocent. Hatred, resentment and envy rival our homes in the quests for more. The appetites of which can not be satisfied. Our houses are no longer homes, in our quests for materialism. No one spends time there and no one feeds their families. We are too busy trampling the sacred part of our lives to find any quality in our being. A smile or common courtesy can no longer be found. Laziness and depression looms, as no one comprehends their purpose for living.

Some one must sound the horn of warning for everyone to hear. There is a war going on, and your family is its' prey. (Jer. 5:26) So many traps have been already set. Subtle is the allure. The snare begins with a word or deed, or even a thought from within. Acceptance of the bait leads to uncharted, unwanted ensnarement. Once the tangled web has been weaved around us, the need for Divine Intervention is all that can dispel us from the net that entrapped us. So watch, look and listen the battle can come close. In contrast a good soldier will encamp his Master, as his Head. (Col. 1: 15-18) With His guidance and direction the trap spring is empty. True wisdom from above has been granted and safe passage in His love. (Job 11:13-20)

THE LOVE OF GOD THAT
TRANSENDS ALL OUR BORDERS

What would happen to the world in which we lived, if Americans and their companies begun to operate in God's love and obedience to His principals? The Bible makes it clear that God is the giver of all things. Everything belongs to God first. Christians serve a Wealthy God. He owns it all! The Bible proclaims us to be the heir and co-heirs with Christ. (Rom. 8: 12-16) As such, we can by faith tap into the resources of God. God is more than pie in the sky; He has the greatest spiritual wealth as well! The greatest command that has been given to us is to love. Love God with all our being and others the same. What a difference would be seen if Americans were committed to showing their love for God and it showed in their love for others. The golden rule of treating others like you would like to be treated, would transform the work place all over the world. The love of God would reach the world over by our daily contacts. From our telephone, to e-mails, His love could reach every countries borders. The American dream of peace, freedom and love would have a good chance of impacting the world. Joy would be a trail easily explained, when an admiring prospect inquired. The blessing of God would abound because of right hearts and relationships. Judgment from God would not have to be feared, for God would live among us and reign in our hearts. His love and attributes of grace, peace, patience, kindness, hope, goodness and joy would be clearly seen in our thriving culture. The results would definitely transcend all our borders.

It sounds like a fairy tale doesn't it? The fact is, that God is in the transforming business. He will be in all that we allow Him to. But, God is not an intruder or un-welcomed guest of hearts. Where God is barred, He will not be found. Free will given to us by our Master will not be an invaded space. The truly wise of this world know God and all of His benefits. (Ps. 103: 2-6) This wisdom is spiritual, but it affects all of a person's life. It can be displayed by the Christian living in Lordship. They will willingly lay down their carnal hearts and minds to Him. For them to live is Christ. (Phil. 1: 20-21) By His Transforming Presence, their lives mirror their Father, Who is God. May it begin with you and I today. May He take us to the next level with Him. It is in our obedience that the world around us, is made a better place. Oh, that we would not sell out our Christian Heritage that is given to us by the blood of the Lamb and our own mankind! Rise up Americans, all of you have something special to give. May you be found faithfully using your talents and abilities to serve our God by serving others. Will you shine out the Light of Love to your brothers in need? May His Purpose, His Glory and His Image be found radiating through you for the whole world to see!

WORDS TO REMEMBER . . . .
UNTIL WE MEET AGAIN!

Love like there is no tomorrow; for this fulfills
the very essence of the Gospel.

Pray with all your being for God hears you!

Believe and you will receive from the Heavenly Lord of Glory above!

Walk confidently knowing your God is with you every step of the way.

TRY . . . put your best efforts behind your prayers;
and be doers of the Word.

Surrender daily . . . first things first . . . for He is worthy of you!

Surrender your burdens daily, as you in faith lay them at His feet!

Prayer is the most powerful thing on earth you can do for someone!

Take time to be still and know your God . . . for He waits for you!

Never forget who is in charge, for He is able
to do more than you can ask!

Reflect on past victories, for they are the "stuff"
that makes courage well up in you!

Praise Him in your discomforts, for He has the power to heal you!

Thank Him for every trial, for when you do . . .
you have in faith given it over to Him!

Walk in peace with everyone for the sake of
Christ, for this is pleasing unto Him!

Search out and stand on the glorious promises,
for they are full of power over you!

Take time to minister to the hurting, for that is
when you look most like God on earth!

Pray for God's will and agenda on earth for
every believer and every church!

Reach in salvation to the lost and dying for this is eternal life to them.

Draw near to God and He will draw near to you!

Exalt and Praise the Lord Jesus and He will lift you up!

Always remember to rely on His Authority,
Victory, Great Power and Grace!

Speak the All Mighty Name of Jesus over all
things; He has all power on earth/heaven.

PRAYERS AND BLESSINGS TO PASS ON

PRAYER FOR DAILY VICTORY:

Dear Lord Jesus,

I surrender to You today, for You are worthy of me. Cleanse me from all my sins. Fill me up to over flowing with Your Spirit and Power. Use me today as Your vessel. Live thru me. Love thru me. Give me Your heart and mind that I may do Your will. Let me have Your eyes and ears that I may see and know all that You have for me to do today. Take my hand Lord and You lead. Let my sin nature be crucified with Christ, as I give Your Spirit control. Lead me safely on the path of adventure and promise today. Watch over and keep my family, friends and all that I love. Thank you Lord for You are able and willing. May Your will be done as I serve You today. May I do all things as unto You! In the All Powerful Name of Jesus I pray! Amen!

PRAYER FOR THE CRISIS TIMES:

Dear Lord Jesus,

You know _____. (state the problem) I pray that You will supernaturally intervene by the power of the Name of Jesus. Lord You have been given all authority on earth and in heaven. (Mat. 28:18) Please _____ (state request) Thank You for what You will do. Thank You that You are willing to help me! Lord we watch for You as we lay these things at your feet. Refresh us Lord and come near us with Your Presence. Let us feel Your Presence as we trust in You. Your Word says that when we trust in You, we shall not be disappointed. Thank you Lord, that You are true to Your Promises. Thank you Lord in advance for all that You will do. We will watch for you. (Isa. 21:6, Luke 5:13, Eph. 1:22-23, Ps. 145:13, Isa. 45:17) In the All Mighty Name of Jesus I pray. AMEN!

PRAYER OF BLESSING FOR YOU!

May you all go in His peace and love. May you know the thrill of His Presence daily, as you surrender your lives to Him. May you experience His victory, power and Presence, over your lives and those you love. Read this book and find all the Scriptures that are waiting for you. May His Word transform you, as you do. Love others and share this book with those you know, that are in need. May God's love and light shine, on all your paths. May He keep you in His love, peace and Presence until we meet one day in heaven!

MY SPIRITUAL JOY CHECK LIST

I have accepted Christ as my Personal Savior.

I pray daily and often.

I practice my faith by being obedient to God's Word.

I share my faith with others.

I care enough to check on the salvation of others.

I listen to those who are hurting.

I help to feed the hungry and clothe the poor.

I actively serve in the church.

I know my spiritual gift and am using it to serve God and others.

I choose to take time for spiritual growth.

I care enough to teach my children about God.

I take my children/family to church.

I take the time to encourage others.

I lift up in prayer those around me.

I am a seeker of Truth and make time for Bible study.

I try to always walk in peace with everyone.

I know and practice unity with the body of Christ.

I walk in love for God and show others His love.

I know the value of praising the Lord, for He is worthy!

I resist the temptation of arguing.

I resist sin by the Power of the Name of Jesus.

I recognize Jesus Authority over all things in heaven and on earth.

I pray by the Authority of the Name of Jesus.

I take time to share what the Lord has done for me.

I give my time and money to the Lord for His work on earth.

I allow Jesus to minister through me to others.

I allow the Spirit to work and speak to others around me.

I stand in faith always.

I keep watch over my heart and mind for Jesus sake.

I watch over my tongue, attitudes and actions for the sake of Jesus.

I confess my sins to keep the channels clear to God.

For Christ sake and the sake of my relationship to Him, I will remain obedient.

I give Christ first place in my life.

I will have a trusting and thankful heart for God.

I stay in hope and faith and never give up.

I lay my burdens down at the feet of Jesus, who is faithful and cares for me.

When I fail, I will get up, dust myself off and continue for His Namesake.

I will forgive others as Christ has forgiven me.

I will always remember that I must forgive myself and move on.

I will remain faithful in trust even when it looks like everything has fallen apart.

I will remember for life Romans 8:28 and live by the truth there.

I will allow the Spirit to be my Power Pack daily, so that I will know victory.

I will stay with God always and serve Him until He takes me with Him to heaven.

My heart wishes to thank Dr. Charles Earl. He provided editing for my book. May God bless and keep you and yours always in His loving care! Your gift serves not only God but America as well! Thank you Lord!